CAREERS IN SECRETARIAL AND OFFICE WORK

Alexa Stace and
Vivien Donald

Fourth Edition

KOGAN PAGE

Copyright © Kogan Page Ltd 1980, 1984, 1986, 1988

All rights reserved. No reproduction, copy or transmission of this publication may be made without written permission.

No paragraph of this publication may be reproduced, copied or transmitted save with written permission or in accordance with the provisions of the Copyright Act 1956 (as amended), or under the terms of any licence permitting limited copying issued by the Copyright Licensing Agency, 7 Ridgmount Street, London WC1E 7AE.

Any person who does any unauthorised act in relation to this publication may be liable to criminal prosecution and civil claims for damages.

First published in Great Britain in 1980 by Kogan Page Limited, 120 Pentonville Road, London N1 9JN
Second edition 1984
Third edition 1986
Fourth edition 1988

British Library Cataloguing in Publication Data

Stace, Alexa
  Careers in secretarial and office work.
  — 4th ed.
  1. Office work — Career guides —
  I. Title   II. Donald, Vivien, *1938*–
  651'.023

  ISBN 1–85091–559–8

Printed and bound in Great Britain by
Richard Clay, The Chaucer Press, Bungay

Contents

Introduction   7
Qualities Required 8

Part 1

1. **Clerical Work**   10
   Wage Clerks 11; Training 12

2. **Typists**   14
   Shorthand-Typists 14; Audio-Typists 16;
   Word Processors 17

3. **Secretarial Work**   20
   Salaries 21; Specialist Secretaries 25;
   Personal Secretaries 28

4. **Employment Agencies**   31

5. **Applying for a Job**   36
   Letter of Application 36; Curriculum Vitae 37;
   The Interview 39; Accepting a Job 41; Contract of
   Employment 41

6. **Office Machines**   42
   Electronic and Correcting Typewriters 43;
   Information Processors 44; Document Printers 44;
   Double-Sided and Self-Collating Copiers 44;
   Teleprinters 45; Fax (Facsimile) Machines 45;
   Accounting Machines 45; Word Processors 46;
   Computers 46

Part 2

7. **Qualifications and Courses Available**   48
   Royal Society of Arts 48; London Chamber of Commerce and Industry 54; Pitman Examinations Institute 64; Business and Technician Education Council 69; Scottish Vocational Education Council 74; The Regional Advisory Councils 85; Specialist Courses 87; The Association of Legal Secretaries 92; Association of Medical Secretaries, Practice Administrators and Receptionists 97; Courses for Farm Secretaries 107; Youth Training Scheme 108; Employment Training 110

Introduction

Office work covers an amazing variety of jobs, from personal assistant to wages clerk, from computer operator to telephone receptionist. Most people, when they think of office work, imagine it in terms of shorthand and typing, but in fact, the variety of jobs is almost endless. The increasing use of machines, together with the microchip revolution, has meant an enormous change in office routines. Machines are increasingly used for many of the office 'chores', such as filing, typing large quantities of envelopes and letters for bulk mailings, updating reports and making copies of lengthy memoranda.

This book aims to give school-leavers (and those who would like to retrain) some idea of the range of opportunities available, and to show them that 'working in an office' need not mean pounding a typewriter all day (electric typewriters don't need pounding anyway), breaking off from time to time to make tea for the boss. One of the most encouraging things about office work is that there are tremendous opportunities for 'getting on' and improving your qualifications while working. Most firms, at whatever level they take you on, will be only too happy to encourage you to improve your skills, whether it is learning typing, improving your speeds, doing a course in office accounts, learning to operate a computer terminal or a word processor, or finding out how a switchboard works.

There is a tremendous range of courses available in office work, and every college in the country runs full-time, part-time and evening courses. It would need a much bigger book than this to list every single course available — there are so many. What we have done is list the main examining bodies, with the qualifications they offer: most colleges offer examinations aiming at these qualifications. Wherever you live, from the outer Hebrides to the remote fastnesses of Wales, you will be in reach of a college offering clerical and secretarial courses in many fields and at varying levels. The problem is not finding a course, but choosing the right one for you from the vast number available.

There are possibilities you may never have considered because you never even knew they existed. As well as normal secretarial courses, there are specialised ones to enable you to work on a large farm dealing with the accounts, for example, or perhaps in a hospital administration department. There are courses for linguists (including one in Welsh) and courses for those who want to work in the law or medicine.

The scope in office work in fact is almost endless. You can work in banking or insurance, in universities, colleges or schools, in the Civil Service or local government, in publishing, travel agencies or solicitors' offices. If you like the security of a large organisation you can try the Civil Service or one of the large commercial firms, which usually have their own training schemes. On the other hand, if you would prefer to be a big fish in a small pond, find a job with a local firm. The smaller the office, the larger the variety of jobs you will be expected to turn your hand to, from making the tea to learning how to operate the switchboard.

Qualities Required

The successful secretary or clerk needs to be methodical and tidy-minded, with a liking for routine. You should also have a strong sense of responsibility, a real interest in seeing the work of the office being done neatly and efficiently, and a sense of loyalty both to your immediate employer and to the firm. You should have a good standard of English, preferably to GCSE/GCE O level pass or CSE Grade 1 level, and the shorthand-typist in particular should be good at spelling and punctuation. Your boss may turn out to be bad-tempered, moody, excitable or even given to flying into rages when things go wrong, so it is important to be calm and unflappable, able to cope with other people's moods philosophically. If you get easily upset by criticism or unpleasantness, you are unlikely to survive office life for long.

NB. *For the sake of simplicity we have referred throughout to the typist or secretary as 'she' and the employer as 'he' but this should not be taken to imply sexual role-casting. You will find plenty of female employers and male clerks and secretaries in the business world too.*

Part 1

Chapter 1
Clerical Work

Clerical work varies widely from office to office, depending on the size of the organisation. It will probably involve some typing and filing and a knowledge of elementary accounts work is always an advantage. Large organisations such as major industrial firms, hospitals, local authorities etc usually have a central filing system employing a number of filing clerks.

In any organisation it is important to be able to refer to documents or correspondence quickly as required. There are a variety of filing systems — alphabetical, subject filing, numerical filing (where an index relates the number to the customer or subject), decimal filing (as used in public libraries), chronological filing (filing documents according to date) etc. All that matters is that the system should be simple to operate, so that papers don't get mis-filed, easy to get at and capable of being expanded as the firm grows.

Most clerks going to a new job will probably find that there is a well-organised system already in existence. But if you go to a fairly new or rapidly expanding firm you may find that you will be asked to set up your own, new filing system.

Local government departments employ a tremendous number of clerks who are often involved in dealing with the public: their work may involve schools, library services, community health or street-sweeping. Whatever the field, they will be employed in sending out and processing forms and other correspondence and keeping detailed records and accounts.

Clerks are employed in travel agencies, in the booking offices of airlines, shipping companies and the railway system. Goods transport too, whether by sea or by haulage firm, also needs clerks to keep records, work out routes and charges and operate timetables.

Clerical Work 11

Wages Clerks

All businesses employ wages clerks. A small firm might have only one wages clerk while a large organisation will have a whole department to deal with wages and salaries. You need to be a calm, methodical person with a definite mathematical bent to be good at this kind of work. Wages sheets, especially where employees are paid hourly or piecework rates, are very complicated and often bonuses or expenses have to be added. In addition, there are PAYE (Pay As You Earn), National Insurance and pension fund contributions to be worked out and deducted from the total amount. A Tax Deduction Card has to be kept for each employee. You will have to use the Tax Tables supplied by the Inland Revenue to work out each employee's taxable pay. Only after all these calculations have been made do you know the final total for each employee's pay packet. If employees are paid in cash the total amount required must be worked out and drawn out of the bank in advance. Alternatively, the wages clerk will arrange for cheques to be drawn or for the bank to pay the money due to employees direct into their bank accounts. Much of the work in accounts and wages departments is now done by adding machines, accounting machines, calculators or even by computer. If a lot of the firm's accounting is done by computer you will probably be trained on the job in how to feed data into the computer and how to obtain information from it, such as statements and invoices.

Qualities Needed

- A tidy, methodical mind.
- A liking for routine and order.
- A reasonable standard of general education. A qualification in maths is an advantage if you want to work in an accounts department.
- A pleasant manner and a willingness to take orders.
- An interest in improving your qualifications through day-release or evening classes.

Checklist of the Clerk's Duties

- Open and distribute incoming mail. This may entail using a letter-opening machine.
- Organise the outgoing mail, either stamping and posting it herself or taking it to the postroom. She may be required to use a franking machine.

- Operate duplicating and addressing machines.
- File correspondence.
- Process orders sent through the post and see they are dealt with promptly.
- Deal with remittances sent through the post — postal orders, cheques etc.
- Keep a petty cash account for small office purchases such as stamps, tea, coffee etc.
- Type out invoices for goods sent out or have the invoices printed out by the computer if there is one.
- Do the accounts work necessary or feed the relevant data into the computer.
- Take cheques and cash to the bank and see that the amount is entered in the firm's paying-in book.
- Do the payroll every week or month, working out PAYE and National Insurance contributions.
- Answer the phone, take messages and deal with clients or customers.

Training

It is possible to start at 16 straight from school as the office junior, but it is an advantage to have taken commercial subjects at school or to take a one-year commercial course at college before starting work. Wages clerks will be expected to have at least GCSE/GCE O level maths. Large organisations often have their own training schemes — either way you will probably be expected to learn how to type. You will also be expected to learn how to operate duplicators, addressing machines, calculators and any other equipment.

Prospects

The growing use of office machinery, streamlining office procedure, and in particular the development of information processors which can store records and information on magnetic cards or tape, is reducing the demand for clerks in the larger organisations. In the smaller office, where the clerk is often jack-of-all-trades, the demand is likely to continue.

Courses

The Royal Society of Arts, the major examining body, offer examinations at three stages:

Examination at Stage I (Elementary), which is below GCSE/GCE O level, in: Office Practice, Bookkeeping, Computers in Data Processing, Cost Accounting, Mathematics, Numeracy, Typewriting.

Examination at Stage II (slightly above GCE O level) in: Accounting, Computers in Data Processing, Cost Accounting, Numeracy, Office Practice, Typewriting.

Examination at Stage III (A level standard) in: Accounting, Commerce (Finance), Cost Accounting, Typewriting.

The RSA also offer a Pre-Vocational (Clerical) course for those interested in office work.

Pitman offer a range of courses in Bookkeeping and Accounts, Commerce and Arithmetic, Computers (Elementary) and Word Processing. They also offer courses designed for the specific needs of companies for their personnel.

A wide variety of colleges offer evening and part-time day courses leading to these exams. Further education colleges also offer their own courses.

The BTEC (Business & Technician Education Council) courses held at further education colleges lead to First, National, Higher National and Continuing Education awards of Certificates and Diplomas. First courses in Business and Finance include numeracy and finance subjects and are designed for junior employees and trainees, especially those involved in clerical, secretarial and office-based work. Courses combine on-the-job training and day-release and block-release courses at a local college. National award courses also include a finance module.

Chapter 2
Typists

Typists are generally employed to type out documents and reports which may be handwritten or typed in draft form. This is called copy-typing and it obviously requires great accuracy as well as speed and commonsense. Typists should also be able to prepare masters or stencils for duplicating machines and be able to operate a duplicator. In a small office, the typist will be expected to do many other jobs as well: filing, running the switchboard, dealing with personal callers and salesmen.

If you are employed by a very large firm you will probably find yourself working with a group of other people in a central office or typing pool under the direction of a supervisor. All correspondence, reports and documents required by the various departments are sent to the typing pool where the supervisor distributes the work. The work consists solely of typing and is suitable for the typist who is very fast and accurate. You are unlikely ever to meet the people whose letters and reports you are typing, so it is not a job for those who like personal contact with the people for whom they are working.

Shorthand-Typists

The work of the typist and the shorthand-typist often overlaps, the basic difference being that the shorthand-typist first takes down work dictated to her then types it out. Again accuracy is vital, but a good command of English is the most important quality. You will have to be able to do your own punctuation and you will find that not everyone is good at dictation. Your boss is quite likely to give you a brief note and expect you to compose a letter from it; equally he might give you a long rambling explantion of what he wants and leave you to frame it how you like. Tact and diplomacy are obviously required! You will have a much greater opportunity than the copy-typist to become involved in your work and in the people above you. If you are good, your boss will come to rely on you heavily, and may even leave you do deal with much of the routine correspondence on your own initiative.

The shorthand-typist is usually employed to work for one or two people and you will soon come to know them and how they like their work to be done. You will have to get used to all sorts of little foibles, such as people wandering round the office while dictating, or interspersing letters with all sorts of sarcastic comments that are not meant to be included.

If you have any doubts about your dictation, make sure you clear them up at once. If you didn't hear a certain phrase clearly, or if something doesn't seem to make sense, it is much better to clear up the problem on the spot.

Qualities Needed

- ☐ A methodical, orderly mind.
- ☐ A good command of English, particularly spelling and grammar.
- ☐ A liking for routine and order.
- ☐ A sense of initiative.
- ☐ A sense of responsibility.
- ☐ Commonsense.
- ☐ Willingness to stay late if required to finish off important letters.
- ☐ Punctuality.

Checklist of the Typist's Duties

- ☐ Look after her typewriter and know how to clean it.
- ☐ Be able to cope with modern typewriters such as electric typewriters, magnetic tape or card typewriters as well as the various attachments to typewriters such as front feed devices, card-loading devices and machines where the paper is fed in continuously.
- ☐ Take dictation and be able to use a dictating machine.
- ☐ Be able to type tabular statements and financial records.
- ☐ Be able to cut stencils, often used when a large number of pages are to be duplicated.
- ☐ Order new stationery when required.

Training

A junior shorthand-typist should have taken a commercial course at school, followed by a one-year college course. You will be expected to have shorthand at 80/100 wpm and typing at 35/40 wpm. You should also have a reasonable command of English and have studied accounts, secretarial duties etc. See Part 2 for details of courses available.

The BTEC First Courses in Business and Finance include Using Information Technology, Information Processing, Keyboarding, Word Processing and Information Transcription. National Award courses in Secretarial Studies include option modules in Audio-Transcription, Keyboarding and its Application, Secretarial Services, Typewriting (including Audio-Typewriting) Transcription and Word Processing.

The Royal Society of Arts offer a series of awards in shorthand at speeds from 80 wpm up to 160 wpm and typewriting in Stages I to III as well as shorthand-typewriting in Stages I to III.

Pitman also offer a series of courses in shorthand and typewriting skills. See Part 2 for details of courses available.

What Kind of Shorthand?

Courses for shorthand-typists are now offered not only in Pitmans' New Era but also in Pitman 2000, Pitmanscript, Teeline and Speedwriting. Which one should you opt for? Basically, Pitman's New Era is the traditional shorthand learned by shorthand-typists, and it is also the fastest. Pitman 2000 is a shorter, simpler system and Pitmanscript, Teeline and Speedwriting are simpler still (but not so fast). If you don't want a job where you will be taking a lot of dictation, or if shorthand will not be primary in your qualifications, one of the simpler (and slower) methods would be sufficient. But many jobs will still demand the conventional shorthand skills and speeds.

Audio-Typists

The audio-typist has a much lonelier job than the shorthand-typist. She types letters and documents, not from shorthand notes, but from tapes made by people she may never have met. The tape is played back on a machine through headphones and she types the letter/document/report straight on to her typewriter. It is a job that requires a lot of concentration and is most suitable for people who don't mind working on their own.

Qualities Needed
The audio-typist needs the qualities listed on p 15 for the shorthand-typist, *plus:*
- Good hearing.
- Good concentration.
- A calm, self-reliant personality.
- The ability to work by herself.

Training
Pitman, the Royal Society of Arts, the London Chamber of Commerce and the various Regional Bodies all offer examinations in audio-typing. There is also a BTEC General First and National Award in Business and Finance audio-typing and audio-transcription. SCOTVEC National Certificate in courses in Office Skills have modules in audio-typing. See p 48 onwards for details of courses.

Word Processors
Many firms increasingly make use of word processors to help to simplify the work of the office. The word processor makes it much easier to cope with the typing of lengthy documents, routine mailings etc, where there may be many alterations.

A word processing program can be used on most microcomputers, but a dedicated word processor cannot usually undertake other tasks.

The machine basically consists of a keyboard, a screen on which you can see what you are typing, a systems unit, and a printer which prints out the final copy when it is ready. The keyboard is that of the conventional typewriter, plus extra instruction keys for deleting, inserting, recalling copy you have already produced, 'finding' copy that has been stored, and for printing out however many copies are required. Corrections, alterations and additions are made by 'calling up' on the screen the relevant line or page and then correcting the text by pressing the relevant keys. Headings can be centred or ranged left at the touch of a key.

The machine can produce personalised letters by merging text already stored with a file of names and addresses held in its memory. The memory can be used as a filing system and reduces the need for paper files. Selected information can be withdrawn from the memory store.

There are spell checking programs which will pick out words

which are not in the memory, so you can confirm the correct spelling.

Some screens enable the operator to look at more than one document at a time.

It is obvious that word processing has virtually endless possibilities and some people are happy to work on it exclusively.

Qualities Needed
A word processor operator who does nothing else in her job may sit all day in front of her machine, producing copy, or she may just use it whenever there are letters or documents to be typed. It needs a lot of concentration and some people find the screen (like a small television screen) tiring to the eyes. A rest period from the screen of 10 minutes in any one hour's operation is probably advisable.

Training
Pitman offer qualifications in Word Processing at Elementary and Intermediate levels, and Word Processing – Theory and Practice. They also offer a Certificate in Practical Word Processing. Many secretarial colleges (such as Sight and Sound) also offer courses in word processing.

Many large firms also organise their own courses, so it is not absolutely necessary to have acquired a qualification before looking for a job. All you have to do is demonstrate a willingness to learn. It will be a definite plus for you if you show enthusiasm for the 'new technology' and are willing to be trained.

Case Study
Julia works for a firm that sells microcomputers, so she was already familiar with the new breed of office machines, and the skills needed to operate them, when she was asked to learn how to operate a word processor.

> I was given a day's training by the manufacturer, and after that I taught myself. It really is very easy if you are determined not to be frightened by the mechanics of the thing. I reckon two weeks' intensive training would be enough to learn how to operate one really efficiently. Now I have to demonstrate how to use them to other girls. The thing that seems to puzzle people most is the business of storing information on floppy discs — they often find it hard to grasp that this is what they have *produced* and the information can be found whenever they want it. Once you have got used to the idea, calling up material stored on a disc is a lot faster than going through a filing

cabinet. You can suffer from eye strain if you sit in front of a word processor all day; however, machines now have an anti-glare screen, so that problem seems to have been solved. Everyone doing secretarial training should learn how to use one in my opinion.

Chapter 3
Secretarial Work

You have only to look at the 'Secretarial Appointments' page of a newspaper to realise that the secretary's job can vary enormously from job to job. In some, the job advertised as a secretary's will turn out to be for a glorified shorthand-typist, paid to sit in the boss's outer office looking impressive and efficient. In others, the job can turn out to be for a high-powered personal secretary to a managing director. The difference is that you can land the first job straight from secretarial college, while the other will demand not only previous experience but also fairly impressive academic qualifications as well, possibly to degree standard.

The secretary usually works for one (possibly two) people. She will be expected to do shorthand and typing (though there may be a junior to do routine typing as well) but the job involves a lot more.

The secretary is expected to take incoming calls for her boss and be able to decide what is important and what is unimportant, dealing with the unimportant or routine calls herself. In other words, she has to judge when to use her initiative and when to refer things to her boss — something that only comes with experience. She also has to use her initiative when it comes to coping with the mail — opening letters and deciding which ones she can answer and which ones will have to be referred to the boss. She will draft replies to the routine letters and present these for signature.

She also has to organise meetings, at anything up to boardroom level. This means informing the secretaries of the other people involved, booking rooms and possibly ordering meals, preparing agendas and documents, taking minutes and typing them up afterwards.

The secretary is also expected to make all travel arrangements for her boss. This can involve booking transatlantic flights, hotel rooms, conference rooms, arranging currency etc, and possibly ringing branch offices abroad. It calls for a good head for detail and endless patience.

To be a good secretary you need to be calm, efficient and unflappable, with a good telephone manner and pleasant personality. You have to be willing to work long hours when necessary and to take on responsibility when asked.

Salaries

Rates of pay for high-flying secretaries have risen sharply in recent years. In 1988 a salary of £30,000 was being offered by the deputy chairman of one of the country's top companies. They were looking for someone (not necessarily a woman) who could deal with high-level businessmen around the world – which would mean a great deal of travel abroad, often at a moment's notice; somebody with plenty of common sense, good communication skills and probably a graduate. A job of this kind is not a nine-to-five type: social life could be virtually nil, with the secretary expected to be on call 24 hours a day.

Salaries of £20,000 or more a year may be paid to the secretaries of chairmen of some public companies, while only £12,000 or £13,000 may be paid to someone doing the same job for a different company not offering such high salaries. Although salaries continue to be highest in London and the South East because of the more expensive mortgages and cost of living, as many companies relocate to the Midlands and further north, salaries there are rising in proportion.

Experience is a more important qualification for the higher paid jobs than academic qualifications, though these are important in showing the ability to memorise and learn. Running the office takes up more of the top secretary's time than typing (which may take up only two hours a week) and duties could include vetting applicants to a secretarial post or even supervising an office move.

For many secretaries, temping is an alternative to full-time employment, with some agencies offering ante-natal care, sickness and holiday pay to those who have worked for a period with the agency. A temp may take home around £189 per week, but agencies pay different rates. Temping can also be a good way of finding a job and getting to know about a company before taking on a permanent post with them (see page 24). Some agencies also offer advice on security and give extra help to women over 40 who are looking for secretarial work.

Checklist of the Secretary's Duties

- ☐ Open and sort the mail: this may involve the use of a letter-opening machine. She will be expected to deal with routine enquiries on her own.
- ☐ Take dictation from the boss and draft routine letters for his signature.
- ☐ Send out mail. A large organisation will have its own mailroom, but in a small firm the secretary will either have to stick on the stamps herself or use a franking machine. If stamps are used she will probably have to keep a post book as a record of the stamps used.
- ☐ File correspondence and other documents. A large organisation will employ one or more filing clerks but the secretary will still be expected to keep personal files for her employer.
- ☐ Answer the phone. The secretary will usually take all incoming calls for her boss. Part of the job will be dealing with routine enquiries and acting as a 'filter' for other calls, protecting her boss from irritating or unnecessary calls which might waste his time. It is important to have a good telephone manner — pleasant and friendly without being cheeky — and she should have a clear speaking voice. She will have to learn the art of fobbing off people politely and firmly without giving offence. In a large firm with a big switchboard the secretary might have a switchboard in her office to deal with her employer's incoming calls.
- ☐ If her boss is out of the office a lot, she will not only have to answer the phone but also take intelligent messages. It is important to take down accurately the name of the person who rang, the name of their firm, if any, and a short summary of their message. She should also get their phone number so that her boss can ring back if required.
- ☐ Deal with visitors. In a small office the secretary will also be the receptionist, sitting in the outer office probably answering the switchboard too. She will be expected to cope with operating the switchboard, receiving incoming calls and dealing with visitors, all at the same time. In a large firm there will be a main reception desk for callers, but the personal secretary will still have to deal with her boss's callers. It will be her job to decide who should or should not see

her boss — and do it tactfully. Whether the boss is in a meeting, away on a business trip or simply doesn't want to see the caller, she must make suitable excuses and ask the caller to make another appointment. Again, a pleasant manner is obviously essential and tact is important too.

- Keep a desk diary both for herself and her boss, making sure that all appointments are written in. She should also keep a notepad for phone calls that her boss has missed, so that he can decide whom to ring back.
- Make travel arrangements. The secretary will have to make out an itinerary for her boss when he goes on a business trip, listing all his appointments day by day. She will also have to book hotels, arrange train and plane tickets, order hire cars or taxis, organise foreign currency and travellers' cheques and make sure that his passport is in order. It may also involve organising special insurance and finding out if vaccination certificates are required. If he is taking samples of products with him she may have to deal with Customs and Excise officials, making sure that all the necessary forms have been filled in and all formalities completed.
- Draw up the agenda for meetings, take accurate minutes and write them up afterwards to represent fairly but briefly what was said and what was decided.
- Make herself familiar, not only with the concerns of her immediate boss, but with the activities of the whole firm and its subsidiaries.
- It is important to be discreet. She should never discuss her boss's private life with others and she should never talk about any confidential work he may be handling.
- Read trade papers and magazines to keep up with current trends.
- Supervise junior staff and be able to replace them when necessary.
- Be able to draw up graphs or charts for wall display or presentation at meetings.
- Reply to invitations and draft letters and memos which need only be presented for signature.
- One of the most important jobs of a secretary is knowing where to go for information, particularly on:
  — telephone numbers
  — spelling/grammar/punctuation

- the correct way of addressing or writing to people, particularly foreigners and titled people
- train and plane timetables and shipping guides
- road travel, hire firms and garages
- hotels
- restaurant and banqueting facilities
- trade and professional publications
- foreign countries
- government departments, other companies
- legal or medical information.

Training

There is no set training for a secretary. It depends very much what age you are and qualifications you have when you start and which course you follow. The Secretarial Skills option in the BTEC National Award equips the student to be a competent secretary with skills in shorthand, typewriting/audio-typewriting. Both the London Chamber of Commerce and Pitman offer options in Word Processing or Information Processing — a skill that is becoming increasingly required.

There are numerous college courses available leading to their own certificates and diplomas, the BTEC and SCOTVEC awards and the awards of the Royal Society of Arts, the London Chamber of Commerce and Pitman. If you have left school at 16 with GCSE/GCE O levels, you can take a two-year secretarial course. If you have one or more A levels, you can do a shorter course. Students with degrees will take a three- to nine-month intensive course. Courses can usually be full-time, part-time or evening. There are also numerous private secretarial colleges which offer their own qualifications. See p 48 onwards for details of courses available.

Case Study

Fiona is secretary to the group editor in a publishing firm; and one of the many people who enter secretarial work more or less by accident. At school she wanted to have a career in music; she comes from a musical family and started to play the piano at the age of five. She took her A levels (in music, English and German) and went on to take a degree in music at a polytechnic.

> I loved being a music student — I enjoyed every minute of it. It was always my great ambition to join an orchestra, but I soon realised that I wasn't good enough for the topflight ones, and I wasn't interested in anything second-best. So straight after my degree I went off to Leeds

Polytechnic to do a secretarial course.

My first idea was to find a job where I could use my music — in a music publishing house for example. But a suitable job just didn't come up and in the end I went to the Jobcentre in Kensington and did a series of 'temping' jobs. I had some very varied jobs — I worked for an engineering firm for three months (until they went bust); I worked at the Hyde Park Hotel; I worked for a solicitor and for a computing firm. The most interesting job of all was typing a film script. I had to do the typing at the scriptwriter's home and I found the script fascinating. I still do some work for him now and then, though not through the agency.

After that I decided to try a secretarial agency and actually found a job in publishing. I had been there two years when I saw an advertisement for the job I had always wanted — PA to the managing director of a music publishing firm. I applied, and was even offered the job. But I turned it down because I didn't like the people. The people you work with are the most important thing about a job, and I knew I wouldn't be happy because I didn't like the person who would have been my boss.

I have been in this job for two years now and I love it. It's very informal, and secretaries are not exploited in the way they are in some other firms. It's well paid and I don't really have any ambitions to go over to the editorial side.

I would advise anyone starting now to temp to begin with. That way you can experience many different jobs and see which suit you. If you are good at your job, with a pleasant manner and a good telephone manner especially, employers will want you.

Specialist Secretaries

Farm Secretaries

Modern farming is very much a business and the farm secretary helps the farmer to cope with the vast amount of paperwork that this entails. You have to fill in forms (including VAT forms), keep records, do accounts, do the wages for the employees, including working out PAYE and National Insurance contributions, and deal with correspondence and filing. If it is a big farm, you will probably be employed full-time. Otherwise, you can be employed by an agency and sent out to various farms as required. You need to be not only efficient in this job but also self-confident and good at working on your own as the farmer is likely to be far too busy to give you much guidance on the paperwork.

Training
Many colleges offer specialist courses on this subject, usually lasting two years. Contact your local education authority for details of courses in your area.

Legal Secretaries

Legal secretaries are employed in solicitors' or barristers' offices, coping with the vast amount of paperwork involved in legal work. The work is obviously highly confidential, so an employer has to be confident that you are entirely reliable and trustworthy before taking you on.

The secretary has to know how to set out legal documents and how to use legal terminology. Legal secretaries may specialise in one particular branch of the law. Having gained experience in that particular branch they then find it fairly easy to find a similar job (there are specialist agencies for legal staff).

Unless you work for a very small firm of solicitors, say in a small country town, you are unlikely to have very much contact with the clients. You will type the letters, lay out the documents, deal with the phone calls, but you are unlikely to become any further involved.

Salaries start at £8,000 and range up to around £11,000.

Training

Many secretaries learn 'on the job', simply starting as a junior in a solicitor's office. This is probably the way most legal secretaries have trained in the past, and there is no doubt that this is a field where practical experience counts for a great deal. But with the present tight job market, more people are taking one of the specialist courses offered by some local colleges of further education, leading to the qualifications of the Association of Legal Secretaries. See page 92 for details.

Case Study

Diane is 26 and a legal secretary; she has just moved down to London from the Midlands. She left the job she originally came down for after only four weeks, because it was too limited, and had just started work with a legal firm in the City.

She always intended to do secretarial work. After taking A levels in history and French she went on to secretarial college for a year where among other awards she gained the London Chamber of Commerce Private Secretary's Certificate. From there she found her first job, in a solicitor's office, and it was there that she learned her trade.

> I've never taken any official qualification in legal secretary work — it's the practical experience that seems to be more important. Once employers know that you've worked in a reputable office for a length of

time — and I was in my first job for five years — they are happy to have you.

Of course, I was spoon-fed to begin with, but they gradually worked me up to dealing with drafting contracts, affidavits and letters, learning the layout and the terminology. Legal documents look baffling to the layman, but it's not so difficult once you begin to understand them. Gradually you learn more and more until you are classed as an experienced legal secretary, and then you have no trouble finding jobs.

My second job was much more responsible and I did a lot of court work — filing in summonses, doing all the paperwork on petty crime cases. It was fascinating, though of course you have very little contact with the clients. The nearest you get to them is answering anxious phone calls, wondering how their case is going.

After two years I decided to broaden my horizons and found a job in London with a firm of solicitors. But they were not very professional so I looked around for something else. Once employers know you have a good few years' solid experience, there is no trouble finding good jobs — or perhaps I have just been lucky. I found this present job through an agency. I had four interviews in one day and three of the firms offered me a job. I chose this one because it's a big, reputable firm doing a lot of company conveyancing, so I'll have the chance to learn something new. They want me to learn how to operate a word processor too, and that will be another plus. I think I'll stick with this firm for a while — they seem very good, the people are friendly and my salary isn't bad at my age!

School Secretaries

All schools employ a secretary who is responsible for the paperwork involved in running a school. The person employed has to be mature and capable, for as well as dealing with attendance records, reports, examination results, correspondence with the local education authority etc, she will probably have frequent contact with teachers, pupils and parents. It is a job demanding tact and discretion as well as the ability to cope sympathetically with small children. There is no special training for this job.

Medical Secretaries

The medical secretary can work in hospital, or in a group practice or health centre, or for an individual doctor, either GP or consultant. Wherever she works, she will have to be familiar with the organisation of the National Health Service and the social services departments, as well as the local health authority. As well as dealing with day-to-day correspondence the job involves a lot of record-keeping, filing and administration. If you are working for a GP or consultant you will have more contact with patients, and tact, patience and a friendly manner are essential here.

Training
Many colleges offer specialist courses, including the two-year course for the Diploma of the Association of Medical Secretaries, for which the entry requirements are four to five GCSE/GCE O level passes. See p 97 for details of courses available.

Bi-Lingual Secretaries/Secretary Linguists
How much the bi-lingual secretary uses her languages depends very much on the job. In some jobs you might hardly use it at all, only translating the odd letter or making phone calls abroad; in others where a firm does a lot of business abroad, you may have to translate incoming mail and compose replies, act as interpreter for foreign visitors, make phone calls abroad, read foreign journals and newspapers and even travel abroad with your boss.

If you have the relevant shorthand there are opportunities for working abroad, though international organisations often require previous experience. The languages most frequently required are French, German and Spanish. It also helps when applying for jobs if you have some practical knowledge of the country.

Training
Again, many colleges offer specialist qualifications, including the awards of the Royal Society of Arts and the London Chamber of Commerce (see p 48 onwards for details of courses). Courses usually last two years and entry requirements in languages are GCSE/GCE O level standard upwards.

Personal Secretaries

The job of the personal secretary is highly responsible. She is expected to work closely with her boss and be able to shoulder a lot of his work. The work is often highly confidential, since the man (or woman) who has a private secretary is fairly high-powered and senior in the firm concerned. Tact and discretion are obviously very important and the secretary should also have a strong sense of responsibility and loyalty to the firm and to her employer. The job can be quite difficult, because she will have to learn to mix with other secretaries and office staff without being 'snooty' and yet at the same time keep silent when office gossip gets round to subjects she happens to know about from the inside.

The personal secretary has in fact to be a paragon of all the virtues, for as well as being the soul of tact and discretion in the office, she will probably also be required to be charming, witty and extrovert in social situations.

The personal secretary will find that she not only has to organise press parties, official receptions, conferences, trade exhibitions etc but take part in them. This may involve acting as 'hostess', taking coats, chatting to new arrivals, offering drinks and snacks and generally keeping things running smoothly. The people she will meet may often be VIPs and she will have to be able to cope with them and their problems without being overawed.

Checklist of the Personal Secretary's Duties
The duties of a personal secretary cover all the points listed in the secretary's duties (p 22). In addition she should:

- Be able to receive and entertain visitors on behalf of her boss.
- Deal with any private matters that will save her boss time and trouble. This can cover anything: buying flowers, collecting prescriptions or laundry, arranging personal appointments, or even meeting his children at railway stations. In the case of a woman boss, she might be asked to make her hair appointments, collect dry cleaning, phone au pair girls etc.
- Arrange all appointments and engagements for her boss.
- Supervise other office staff, replacing them when necessary and ensuring where possible that her boss is not troubled by any trivial staff problems.
- Handle her boss's office or departmental budgeting and accounts.
- If her boss is a public figure she may also have to deal with the press — discretion is obviously vital here.

Training
Royal Society of Arts
The RSA offer a post-A level Diploma for Personal Assistants, intended for top-level personal secretaries or assistants, covering the responsibilities and background knowlege required. See p 48 for details of courses.

London Chamber of Commerce

The London Chamber of Commerce offer a Private Secretary's Certificate and a Private and Executive Secretary's Diploma. The Certificate is intended for secretaries to middle managers while the Diploma is intended for senior private secretaries to top-level managers. For the Certificate candidates must pass in Communications (Use of English), Office Organisation and Secretarial Procedures, Structure of Business, Shorthand-Transcription and/or Audio-Transcription, Interview. For the Diploma candidates must be not less than 20 and must pass in Communication (Use of English), Communication (Shorthand- and/or Audio-Transcription), Secretarial Administration, Management Appreciation, Interview. Both the Certificate and the Diploma have an option in Information Processing.

Holders of the Private Secretary's Diploma are entitled to apply for membership of the Institute of Qualified Private Secretaries, 126 Farnham Road, Slough, Berks SL1 4XA. See p 55 for details of courses.

Higher National Diplomas

The BTEC HND in Business and Finance can be taken with a bias in higher private secretarial duties and skills. Contact your local education authority for colleges running these courses.

Chapter 4
Employment Agencies

Once you are qualified, or on the way to being qualified, how do you find yourself a job? There are various organisations you can approach for help: the Careers Service, your local Jobcentre or employment office and so on. There are also specialised employment agencies which act as a go-between between you and the employer. The agency will interview you, assess your capabilities, and send you to interviews for jobs for which they think you are suitable. It doesn't cost you anything — the employer pays the agency to find suitable staff. Most agencies handle all kinds of office staff — clerks, typists, secretaries etc — though there are a few specialist ones that deal for example with legal secretaries or top-level personal secretaries.

Below is a selection of agencies in major towns up and down the country. Some of the big agencies, however, have branches in almost every town in the country. To find your nearest one, ring the London office or look in your local Yellow Pages under 'Employment Agencies'.

Birmingham Area

Alfred Marks Bureau Ltd, 84 New Street, Birmingham 2; 021-643 2656

Betty Walker Staff Agency, 1206 Stratford Road, Ham Green, Birmingham B28 8HN; 021-777 6416/6592

Brook Street Bureau, 119 New Street, Birmingham 2; 021-643 7404

Kelly Girl, The Rotunda, 92 High Street, Birmingham; 021-632 6391

Pertemps Jobshops, 81–82 Darlington Street, Wolverhampton WV1 4JD; 0902 712345

57 New Street, Birmingham; 021-643 5000

9 Bull Street, Ringway, West Bromwich; 021-525 5151

Bristol Area

Bath Employment Bureau, 7 Quiet Street, Bath; 0225 64463/63868
City Staff Centre, 27 St Stephen's Street, Bristol 1; 0272 298036
Brook Street Bureau, 10 St Augustine's Parade, Bristol; 0272 24552
The Pamela Neave Bureau, 18 St Augustine Parade, The Centre, Bristol; 0272 211831
Sue Sheppard, 2 Park Street, Bristol; 0272 265403/290709

Cambridge Area

Ann Pettengell Bureau, 41–43 Mill Road, Cambridge; 0223 350234
Cambridge Personnel, 23 St Andrews Street, Cambridge; 0223 358675/66561
Royston Staff Bureau, 1 Kilnhouse Yard, Royston, Hertfordshire; 0763 41131

Cardiff & South East Wales

Brook Street Bureau, 53 Queen Street, Cardiff; 0222 397471
Churchills Staff Agency, 57 Charles Street, Cardiff; 0222 26565/397134
Jennifer Griffiths Bureau, 60 Nolton Street, Bridgend; 0656 69370
Manpower, 90 Queen Street, Cardiff; 0222 394721

Leeds Area

Bertram Staff Agency, 104 Briggate, Leeds 1; 0532 442201
Beverley Howard Employment Bureau, 148 Main Street, Shadwell, Leeds 17; 0532 737548/737374
Brook Street Bureau, 17 Albion Place, Leeds 1; 0532 436611
Executemps (Secretarial Services), Minerva House, 29 East Parade, Leeds; 0532 444401
Horsforth Staff Bureau, 60 Town Street, Horsforth, Leeds; 0532 586891
Reed Employment, Landslow, Leeds 1; 0532 439671

Leicester Area

Alfred Marks Bureau, 18 Granby Street, Leicester; 0533 530516
Brook Street Bureau, 49 Gallowtree Gate, Leicester; 0533 56171
Hinckley Secretarial Services, Edwards Buildings, Coventry Road, Hinckley, Leicestershire; 0455 635569
Lutterworth Staff & Secretarial Bureau, 23a George Street, Lutterworth; 04555 56862

Employment Agencies 33

London Area

Many firms have branches all over London. In each case the address and number of the head office is given — ring to find out where your nearest branch is.

ASA Law Secretaries, 31 Cursitor Street, London EC4; 01-404 4990

Acme Agency, 315 Oxford Street, London W1; 01-493 4000

Alfred Marks Bureau Ltd (head office), 84 Regent Street, London W1; 01-437 7855

Brook Street Bureau (head office), Stockley House, 130 Wilton Road, London SW1V 1LQ; 01-630 1311

Chancery Lane Legal Secretaries, 30 Chancery Lane, London WC2; 01-242 1301

Directors' Secretaries Ltd, 27 Old Bond Street, London W1X 3AA; 01-629 9323

Drake Personnel, 225 Regent Street, London W1; 01-734 0911

International Secretaries Ltd, 174 New Bond Street, London W1; 01-491 7100

Kelly Girl, 181 Oxford Street, London W1; 01-734 3511

Rand Services, 37 Margaret Street, London W1; 01-491 3774

Reed Employment Ltd, 181–183 Victoria Street, London SW1; 01-828 3758

Sarah Hodge, 115 New Bond Street, London W1; 01-499 7781

Secretaries Plus, 146 Bishopsgate, London EC2; 01-377 8600

Manchester Area

Alfred Marks Bureau Ltd, 54 Deansgate, Manchester 3; 061-834 6883

Brook Street Bureau Ltd, 98 Market Street, Manchester M1 1PB; 061-832 8135

Kelly Girl, 73 Princess Street, Albert Square, Manchester; 061-228 6681

Reed Employment, 15 Piccadilly, Manchester 1; 061-832 6631

Salford Secretarial Bureau, 235 Chapel Street, Salford M3; 061-832 2331

West Staff Bureau, 6 Bank Street, Bury, Lancashire; 061-764 2303

Mersey Area

Jordans Employment Agency, 62 Bickerstaffe Street, St Helens, Lancashire; 0744 20226

PASS Personnel, 4 Post Office Avenue, Southport, Lancashire; 0704 34021

Placements Recruitment Services, 1 Wynne Road, St Helens, Lancashire; 0744 39592

Rainford Office Services, 8a Ormskirk Road, Rainford;
074 488 3289/4051

Newcastle upon Tyne Area

Alfred Marks Bureau Ltd, 6 New Bridge Street, Newcastle upon Tyne 1;
0632 329673

Brook Street Bureau, 64-68 Northumberland Street, Newcastle upon Tyne NE1 7DF; 0632 325661

Eldon Bureau, 1 Eldon Square, Newcastle upon Tyne 1; 0632 323623

Hardisty & Moulden Executive Services, Collingwood Buildings, Collingwood Street, Newcastle upon Tyne; 0632 321743

Secretarial Services, 49 John Street, Sunderland; 0783 75174

Oxford Area

Alfred Marks Bureau Ltd, 124 High Street, Oxford; 0865 721341

Apex Recruitment Services, 25 Horse Fair, Banbury; 0295 55225

Brook Street Bureau, 16 High Street, Oxford; 0865 722571

Daton Recruitment Ltd, 23 Easton Street, High Wycombe, Buckinghamshire; 0494 30517

Teamwork, 73 High Street, Banbury; 0295 53449

Tunbridge Wells Area

Floss Staff Agency, 103b London Road, Sevenoaks; 0732 459155
  14 Ritz Buildings, Church Road, Tunbridge Wells; 0892 24122

Goodchilds Employment Agency, 48 The Broadway, Crawley, West Sussex RH10 1HG; 0293 26147/25015

Grosvenor Employment Agency, 86a London Road, East Grinstead; 0342 24240/24309

Personnel Selection (Edenbridge) 104a High Street, Edenbridge; 0732 864141

Scotland

Edinburgh

Drake Personnel, 29 Frederick Street, Edinburgh; 031-226 5951

Margaret Hodge Staff Consultants, 10a Cross Wynd, Dunfermline; 0383 736163
  2 Randolph Place, Edinburgh; 031-225 8901

Raeburn Recruitment, 52 Rose Street Lane, Edinburgh; 031-225 5820

Selectstaff, 28 North Bridge Road, Edinburgh; 031-226 5500

Glasgow
Rand Services, 47 Hope Street, Glasgow 2; 041-248 2611
  2 St Mirren Street, Paisley; 041-887 2121
Regent Employment Agency, 96 Miller Street, Glasgow 1;
  041-221 1191

Chapter 5
Applying for a Job

Employing the right strategy can make all the difference to your success in applying for jobs. Being well organised right from the start really will pay dividends. Applying for jobs, filling in application forms and going for interviews can be boring, time-consuming and often very depressing, but you must not allow any of this to affect either your applications or your manner at interviews. *Force yourself* to take the time to compose a good letter of application — a sloppy, badly-written one will only end up in the wastepaper-basket. A good-looking letter is particularly important if you are applying for a secretarial post. Who wants to employ a secretary who can't spell or doesn't know how to lay out a letter correctly? *Force yourself* to take time over your curriculum vitae (see p 38) making sure that it is neat, accurate and has all the relevant facts included. *Force yourself* to think about the interview. If you remember that there is a technique both to holding interviews and to being interviewed, it will help. In this chapter there is a checklist of points to remember for interviews, as well as a short guide to how interviews are conducted, so that you can anticipate questions. Once you have grasped the general pattern of interviews, you will find them less confusing and frightening. And remember, never turn down the chance of going for an interview. The more practice you have at being interviewed, the better.

Letter of Application

- Do a rough draft of the letter first to make sure that you have covered all essential points.
- Give details of your qualifications and experience (your curriculum vitae) on a separate sheet. See p 38 for how to lay out your curriculum vitae.

Applying for a Job

- Make absolutely sure that there are no spelling mistakes or grammatical errors in your letter. If in any doubt, ask a friend to look it over for you.
- Use good quality writing-paper for your letter.
- Keep your letter brief and to the point. Mention where you saw the advertisement.
- Keep a copy of your letter for reference.

Curriculum Vitae

See p 38 for how to lay out your curriculum vitae. It should give:

- full name and address
- date of birth
- schools attended
- examinations passed
- any other honours won at school
- any particular position of authority held at school, eg school captain
- training courses or colleges attended and qualifications gained
- previous jobs held or any other experience gained
- present employment, if any
- names and addresses of two referees. One of these should be a previous employer or someone who has personal knowledge of your capabilities.
- personal interests/hobbies
- languages. If you have adequate written or speaking knowledge of any languages, mention it here.
- If you have a current driving licence mention it here.

Checklist of Points to Remember

Remember that for most jobs your appearance, manner and general level of education will be as important as your typing speeds. General points to bear in mind are:

- Be on time for the interview. If you are even five minutes late it will be a black mark against you, so leave in plenty of time, allowing for traffic jams, trains being late etc.
- Make sure you are well-groomed — no messy hair, dirty shoes, grubby finger-nails.
- Dress neatly rather than flashily. Avoid heavy perfumes, low necklines or very high heels.
- Smile pleasantly and look directly at the interviewer.

MARY BROWN
32 PARK AVENUE, MANCHESTER M3 5AW
Tel: 061-123 4567

DATE OF BIRTH: ....

AGE NOW: ....

SCHOOLS ATTENDED:

   (Name and town)   (From) — (To)

COLLEGES ATTENDED:

   (Name and town)   (From) — (To)

QUALIFICATIONS:

   (Name of examination)   (Subject)   (Grade)

(Include all school/college examinations which you have passed and any other qualifications/certificates you have which you think would be relevant or of interest to employers)

POSITIONS HELD:

INTERESTS AND ACTIVITIES:

FURTHER EDUCATIONAL PLANS:

EXPERIENCE:
(Start with your current job and work backwards)

REFERENCES:
(1) (Name of referee)   (Address) (Tel no)
(2)
(3)

A sample curriculum vitae

- Don't smoke unless invited to do so.
- Speak clearly without mumbling. Don't say 'sort of' or 'you know' every other word.
- Don't giggle or make jokey remarks.
- Be honest about your abilities.
- Never make snide or disparaging remarks about a previous employer.
- Don't allow yourself to get angry or irritated at anything the interviewer says. He may be finding out how well you stand up to pressure. So try to keep cool and unfussed no matter how the conversation goes.
- Don't pick a fight with the interviewer or allow yourself to get into an argument with him, even if you know he is in the wrong.
- Try to avoid giving 'yes' and 'no' answers, but on the other hand don't ramble.
- Remember all the time that you have to sell yourself to the employer. Talk about your good points and what you can do, rather than what you can't do.
- Above all, try to appear interested in the job and the firm. The employer will always prefer someone who seems lively and enthusiastic.

The Interview

You will find interviews less frightening if you remember that all interviews have a form and structure. The interviewer will start by putting you at your ease, making small talk about the weather or the trains and perhaps asking if you smoke. He will then try to draw you out by asking about your career to date, what you have been doing since you left school etc. He wants you to talk so that he can get an impression of what you are like, but beware of rambling on for too long. He will then probably move on to your letter or application form and go over the details. It is important not to become bored or irritated at this point. All the things he is asking may already be there on the form, but tell him again, politely. Have an answer ready when he asks how you see your career developing, or what you would like to be doing in five years time. Be ready too for the question why you are applying for this particular job. Even if you have been sent by an agency you must still make it sound as if you are keen on the job and want to apply for it. He will probably then ask if you have a clear picture of the job and what it entails. This is to see if you have really thought about it. At the end, he will probably ask if you have any questions, and you must try to think of something to say. If it looks as if you are going to be offered the job, this could be the occasion to clear up anything you are not sure about. We give below some points to watch under 'Accepting a Job'. This would be the moment to ask to see the office, if you have not already done so, and to clear up any queries about salary, holidays, pension rights etc.

Telephone Interviews

There is an increasing trend towards telephone interviewing. The employer does his preliminary interview over the telephone and then, if he likes the sound of you, he will ask you to come along for a more formal interview. Or, having gone for a preliminary interview, you may be rung up by the personnel officer for a background chat. In either event, it is most important that you should be well prepared.

Always remember:
- Write out all the relevant details about yourself on a piece of paper in case you become flustered — school, exams passed, qualifications for the job, training courses completed etc.
- Try to speak in a firm, clear voice. Don't mumble and 'um' and 'er' and say 'sort of' or 'you know' every other word. Your voice is the only thing the employer has to go on, so you must try to sound pleasant, self-assured and capable. Take a deep breath and try not to gabble through nerves.
- Come straight to the point. 'I'm ringing about the advertisement in today's paper. It sounds very interesting. Could you tell me more about it please?'
- If you are ringing from a call-box, make sure you have an ample supply of coins.

Checklist of Questions to be Prepared for

The interviewer is sure to ask some, if not all, of these questions — make sure you have answers prepared.

- What made you decide to go in for a secretarial/clerical career?
- What made you apply for this job?
- What makes you think you will be good at this job?
- What particularly attracts you about this job?
- How would you like your career to develop/What would you

like to be doing in five years' time?
- What do you like doing in your spare time?
- Tell me about your family.
- (if you already have a job)
Why do you want to leave your present job?

Accepting a Job

Before you get your contract of employment, before you even write a letter of acceptance, you should make sure you know your position. No one should accept a job without understanding what the job entails, what the hours and rate of pay are and what the holiday entitlement is. If you have any doubts or queries now is the time to clear them up. It is no use saying later that you didn't realise what the job involved, or you thought you were entitled to four weeks' holiday when it turns out to be two.

Contract of Employment

A contract of employment exists as soon as someone offers you a job (even verbally) at a certain rate of pay and you accept. Within 13 weeks of your starting work the employer is required by law to give you written details of your contract. These cover:

- job title
- pay
- how you are paid (weekly, monthly etc)
- hours of work
- holiday entitlement and pay
- length of notice
- disciplinary and grievance procedures
- pension rights
- any requirement to join a specific trade union.

If you are not given a copy of your contract within 13 weeks of joining a firm, you should ask for it. The contract of employment is a legal document, so make sure that you keep it in a safe place.

Chapter 6
Office Machines

Much has been made in the newspapers of the microchip revolution and how it is going to put people out of work but this is really just a matter of opinion. There are as many different opinions on the effect of the 'revolution' as there are pundits, and some people believe that in the long term employment will actually be increased. Certainly, in the USA it is not anticipated that the new technology will seriously cause unemployment.

It is true that in the last few years many machines have appeared which have considerably streamlined office routine, at least in the larger firms: machines that can run off hundreds of copies of a document and collate the pages for you; machines that can run off all the addressed envelopes needed for a bulk mailing; machines that can update information on record cards without the bore of searching through files; machines that can do complicated calculations; and of course the computer that can produce invoices and statements at the touch of a button.

Fewer clerks will be employed, true, but people will still be needed to run the machines, to feed them with data and to cope when (inevitably) they break down or fail to supply the information required. There is little that you can do to prepare for this work, though some courses, such as the BTEC First Award, do cover the use of conventional office machines and equipment, showing you how to use calculators, franking machines, addressing machines etc. But no secretarial course will prepare you for the newer office machines. There are specific courses in computer programming and data processing, but they are quite unnecessary on a secretarial course — in any case you might well find that the firm you go to uses a quite different system or a different computer 'language'. Most firms prefer to do their own training, either sending you on a short course or using the training personnel of the firm that sold them the computer, information processor or whatever.

It is not even necessary to be particularly good at maths for this work. A good all-round education and a capacity for logical thought are all that is required to be a computer operator or a data processor. What is important is to be willing to try out something new and be keen to learn. When your firm acquires a computer or some other complicated piece of machinery, and they have to choose who should be trained to use it — don't shrink back. If you are willing to have a go and acquire whatever new expertise is required, you are unlikely to find yourself out of a job. Operating the keyboard of a visual display unit (VDU) is remarkably like operating an electric typewriter. It helps if you understand how it works, so that you know what to do if it goes wrong, but there is nothing very difficult or out of the way about using such machinery.

In your training you will probably come across the more usual office machines that are now more or less standard equipment in any firm, large or small: electric typewriters, desk calculators, adding machines, franking machines, photocopying machines, and facsimile machines. Once you start work, particularly in a large company, you may come across some of the newer equipment available.

Electronic and Correcting Typewriters

Typewriters have become highly sophisticated instruments. Many now incorporate a two-line self-correcting element, doing away with messy corrections on the paper. When all the required changes have been made (simply by button control) a perfect copy can be produced automatically. Many of these typewriters also have a 'memory' enabling pages of text to be stored for re-use or revision. When the material is required it can be played out automatically in the format specified — and these typewriters can also justify right-hand margin and centre automatically. Other functions that help the typist include automatic paper injection, a search function that finds any word, line or paragraph in a text and replaces it with another (useful for saving time with legal documents or engineering specifications), automatic print-outs of a standard letter incorporating different names and addresses, and stop and message codes to allow different phrases to be inserted during printing; automatic paragraph indentation and 'page end command' that limits the number of lines printed per page and automatically ejects the page — and prints out headings, if required, at the top of the next sheet. Tabulation comes in four forms: normal, decimal, vertical line and vertical tab. Typefaces can be changed to bold, with automatic underlining.

Information Processors

These machines have done away with the need for cumbersome filing systems or card indexes. Now, when a firm wants to update a routine document sent out or do a bulk mailing, the material required can be produced on this machine without any need for lengthy retyping of documents. It works by storing information on magnetic cards — extra items can then be added, deleted, revised or assembled at the touch of a button: there is a display screen (like a TV) to guide the operator through the changes to be made. The machine can be used for processing records, constructing documents from stored text, or updating letters: words, phrases or paragraphs can be amended or replaced as necessary without any further typing having to be done. Any kind of information stored can be turned into reports or lists. To type out the full amended copy the typist presses a button and the final version is produced automatically.

These machines can also be linked to a computer to print out information from the computer or even produce letters and envelopes automatically by merging data from a computer file with information stored on magnetic cards.

Document Printers

These now do most of the chores that used to be done by a copy-typist. They print out letters, envelopes or reports from stored magnetic cards. They can be instructed on the format required, including paragraph indentation, typeface and number of pages.

Double-Sided and Self-Collating Copiers

Photocopying machines have also become much more sophisticated. No one needs to stand for hours at a machine laboriously copying lengthy documents. Automatic copiers can now produce

55 copies a minute. If required these machines can also do double-sided copying, photo-reduce, overlay and collate copies automatically for you, taking a lot of the drudgery out of copying. Some even print in colour.

Teleprinters

These machines, which look like typewriters, are used for sending and receiving urgent messages over the telegraph or phone. The main system is Telex. The operator either types out the message or prepares a punched tape which can then be fed into an automatic transmitter. A printed copy of the message is produced on the teleprinter at the receiving end. Modern telex machines have message memory facilities, automatic dialling for often-used numbers, editing facilities and VDU screens. Calls can be made overseas as well as in the UK and messages can be sent day or night, provided that the receiver is switched on.

Fax (Facsimile) Machines

The next stage on from a telex machine, fax machines transmit copies of documents, plans or text by phone to anywhere in the world; some take only 30 seconds per page. A sheet of paper is inserted into the machine, the image is translated into a series of dots and transmitted along phone lines to be printed out on to another sheet of paper by the receiving machine. Since drawings, or even handwriting, can be transmitted, as well as printed documents, fax machines save a great deal of time; there are no special skills involved in their use.

Accounting Machines

These machines have relieved bookkeepers of much routine work, since they can make several entries automatically, in one operation. The use of magnetic cards in these machines has increased their speed: the cards can be used to store information such as account numbers, balances and names and addresses. They are also invaluable for storing the detailed information required for working out PAYE on a payroll — salary paid to date, tax paid to date, National Insurance contributions etc. Entries are made by feeding in the magnetic cards, and the operator then keys in the data through a keyboard rather like a typewriter.

Storing and updating data on these cards takes a lot of the drudgery out of accounting procedures, particularly since calculations are carried out automatically.

Word Processors

Word processors are highly sophisticated electronic typewriters, with large display screens to help with editing and page layout. The material is not printed out on to a page fed into the machine, as is the case with a typewriter, but printed separately — the typist watches the screen display, instead of the page, during typing. Blocks of text can be added, removed or moved around, to save revision time, and the result can be stored in the memory or printed out.

Word processors can also be used to transmit information to other word processors within a company, or to the company's main computer (electronic mailboxing); transmit, receive or store telex or teletext messages; and can even be converted into a microcomputer, using software to help in business management (revenue and cash flow analysis, sales summaries etc).

Although the display screens of word processors have been criticised in the past as being tiring to the operator's eyes, some are now coloured black and gold, or even black and white, as well as black and green.

Computers

Computers are now used in many offices and businesses to carry out routine accounting calculations, as well as dealing with more complex data. Computers can be used to do payroll calculations, invoicing, costing etc. The point of using the computer is not simply to save the office staff from a lot of drudgery — the computer can do the complicated calculations involved in a fraction of the time it would take to do them any other way.

Data is fed into the computer either in the form of punched cards or magnetic tape, or by typing direct on to a console linked to the machine. Information received from the computer can also be in the form of cards, tape, discs, or it can be displayed on a VDU.

Computer operators or data processors are concerned with preparing material to be 'input' into the computer. Training for this is usually done on-the-job, instruction being given by a representative sent by the manufacturer.

Part 2

Chapter 7
Qualifications and Courses Available

The main examining bodies in the field of secretarial and office work are the Royal Society of Arts, Pitman and the London Chamber of Commerce and Industry (LCCI). Many colleges all over the country offer day and evening courses leading to their examinations. There are also the awards offered by the Business and Technician Education Council and the Scottish Vocational Education Council, the two bodies which are now responsible for organising qualifications in business studies. Contact your local education authority for details of colleges in your area offering these courses.

Royal Society of Arts

8 John Adam Street, London WC2N 6EZ; 01-930 5115

Single-Subject Examinations

Entry Qualifications
None.

For Whom Intended
The Single-Subject examinations are primarily intended for students taking clerical and secretarial courses at colleges of further education. They are also suitable for students following vocational courses of study in schools.

The Board offers examinations at Stage I (Elementary), Stage II (Intermediate) and Stage III (Advanced). Candidates can be any age. You can enter for subjects at any Stage, ie you need not take Stage I of a subject before taking Stage II, or Stage I and Stage II before taking the Advanced.

Qualifications and Courses Available

Accounting Stage II
Accounting Stage III
Audio-Transcription Stage I
Audio-Transcription Stage II
Audio-Transcription Stage III
Audio-Typewriting in French Stage II
Background to Business Stage I
Background to Business Stage II
Background to Business Stage III
Bookkeeping Stage I
Civics Stage I
Commerce (Finance) Stage III
Communication in Business Stage I
Communication in Business Stage II
Communication in Business Stage III
Computer Keyboard Skills
Computer Literacy and Information Technology
Computers in Data Processing Stage I
Computers in Data Processing Stage II
Copy Typing Speed Test
Core Text Processing Skills
Cost Accounting Stage I
Cost Accounting Stage II
Cost Accounting Stage III
Economics – GCSE
Economics Stage III
English Language Stage I
English Language Stage II
English Language Stage III
Keyboarding Applications (Modular) – GCSE
Law and Public Administration Stage II
Mathematics Stage I
Medical Audio-Typewriting Stage II
Medical Shorthand-Typewriting Stage II
Medical Shorthand
Modern Literature in English Stage I
Modern Literature in English Stage II
Numeracy Stage I
Numeracy Stage II
Office Practice Stage I
Office Practice Stage II
Reception Skills (Group Awards only)
Secretarial Duties Stage II
Shorthand in French
Shorthand Transcription Stage I
Shorthand Transcription Stage II
Shorthand Transcription Stage III
Shorthand-Typewriting Stage II
Shorthand-Typewriting Stage III
Statistics GCSE
Typewriting Skills Stage I
Typewriting Skills Stage II
Typewriting Skills Stage III
Word Processing Stage I
Word Processing Stage II

Group Awards

Certificate/Diploma in General Reception
Diploma in Business Studies – Stage II
Diploma in Secretarial Studies – Stage II

These schemes are intended for candidates who wish to obtain a Group Award at Stage II and who have followed a course of instruction appropriate to any aspect of office work.

A 'group' consists of three or four compulsory subjects and at least one optional subject which is specifically related to the particular Group Award for which the candidate has entered. In each subject the same question papers will be used as for the single subject examinations. The principle of the award rests on all the examinations being entered for and passed at the same series. However, failure to meet these requirements will enable candidates to receive single-subject certificates for those subjects in which they have been successful.

Diploma for Personal Assistants

This scheme is intended to represent a very high standard of ability in the secretarial and junior administrative field and it is hoped that it will serve the needs of those aiming at such positions as personal assistants or personal secretaries to senior management or in supervisory posts in office management.

Students will be required to take the following subjects: Administration: Economic and Financial Aspects; Legal Aspects; Personnel and Functional Aspects. Communication: Written, Office Skills Applied, Oral. Students are expected to have at least two A levels or their equivalent.

Language Examinations for Secretaries and Office Workers

Diploma for Bilingual Secretaries

For Whom Intended
Those aiming at entering employment as personal assistants/personal secretaries to senior management in the United Kingdom or abroad.

Entry Qualifications
Candidates usually have a degree in Modern Languages. Alternatively, the Certificate for Secretarial Linguists (see below).

Type of Course
Usually a one-year full-time course in secretarial skills combined with languages.

Content of Examination
(a) There is a partial joint assessment for the two Diploma schemes based on a video presentation of a meeting, and tests of interlingual skills in a business context with appropriate options where applicable. There will be separate oral examinations.
(b) The scheme is offered in French, German and Spanish.
(c) There are optional Foreign Shorthand examinations and Audio-Typewriting in French.

Certificate for Secretarial Linguists

For Whom Intended
Those aiming at entering employment as a secretary in a situation where language skills are needed.

Entry Qualifications
None, although an A level in the language concerned or RSA level 4 Languages for the Office is useful.

Type of Course
Usually one-year full-time course in secretarial skills combined with languages.

Content of Examination
(a) The assessment scheme consists of tasks based on the candidate's role as a secretary, ie tasks such as dealing with answerphone messages, an in-tray and a social/business situation including use of the telephone.
(b) The scheme is offered in French, German, Italian and Spanish.
(c) There are optional Foreign Shorthand examinations and Audio-Typewriting in French.

Certificate in Languages for Business

For Whom Intended
Office workers and management trainees interested in a basic practical qualification in the business use of the language.

Entry Qualifications
Normally GCSE/GCE O level in the language concerned is useful, or RSA Languages for Commercial Purposes (see below).

Type of Course
Usually one-year full-time course in business language, possibly combined with secretarial skills.

Content of Examination
(a) The assessment scheme will consist of tasks based on the candidate's role as a secretary, ie tasks such as dealing with answerphone messages, an in-tray and a social/business situation including the use of the telephone.
(b) The scheme is offered in French, German, Italian and Spanish.
(c) There is an optional endorsement for typing.

Careers in Secretarial and Office Work

Languages for Commercial Purposes

Equivalent for Levels 2 and 3 of the communicative language examinations but dealing specifically with business and commercial contexts.

For Whom Intended

For those already in or intending to enter the sort of jobs in business and commerce where a foreign language is used.

Type of Course

Element of commercial courses in further education, vocational course in school.

The same type of test as for Levels 2 and 3 of general communicative languages using commercial scenarios. Common assessment for two levels with additional elements at Level 3.

General Communicative Language Examinations

From Level 1 (basic survival kit) to Level 4, a practical A level equivalent.

For Whom Intended

For anyone needing to communicate in a foreign language, whether for work or preparation for work (or for pleasure). No entry qualifications but candidates are recommended to take one level before going on to the next. Those with GCSE/GCE O level might attempt Level 3 before Level 4.

Type of Course

Any course where practical communication is the aim of adult education or languages are linked to general vocational courses in schools etc.

Content of Examination

Tests of speaking, listening, reading and writing (writing not at Level 1; optional at Level 2) in realistic contexts.

Integrated Vocational Awards

Vocational Certificate (Clerical)

For Whom Intended

Those interested or involved (eg through YTS) in occupations involving the performance of clerical skills, eg warehouse work, storekeeping, packaging, goods checking, record keeping, and office work.

Type of Course

The Board does not specify the required number of weeks' attendance on the scheme, nor particular patterns of attendance. Trainees can leave, and receive their certificate, at a time appropriate to them.

Course Content

The scheme includes communication, numeracy, career and personal development, handling mail, record-keeping, use of office machinery, telephone and reception skills, security, health and safety. Work is monitored by tutors or supervisors and standards assured by RSA assessors.

Candidates achieving all the compulsory objectives are awarded a profile certificate.

These courses provide a good foundation for business studies courses such as the RSA Diploma in Office Procedures and General Reception.

Certificate/Diploma in Office Procedures

Certificate/Diploma in General Reception

These schemes have been developed to meet a growing demand for a style of course and certification which recognises individual achievement. They are designed for those seeking employment in office work and general reception. The schemes are for students or trainees progressing from Vocational Certificate (Clerical); or already competent in basic skills; or on YTS schemes; or students on full-time courses for office work; or adults returning to work.

The schemes consist of interrelated tasks for office work and general reception. Competence is recorded through an assessment record and monitored by tutors or supervisors.

Pre-Vocational Clerical Course

For Whom Intended

Those interested in office work and wanting to gain employment in junior office positions or going on to further study or training.

Type of Course

This pre-employment course may be run as a short intensive programme with adults, or over two years as part of the option system for 4th and 5th years in school. The course can be combined with full-time study on other subjects in schools and colleges.

Course Content

An integrated course comprising: Communication (oral and written); Numeracy; Clerical Procedures (including keyboarding); Background to Business. The course should include relevant work experience.

Candidates are awarded a profile certificate on the basis of continuous assessment and an optional examination in the form of a folder of practical work may be taken, leading to the endorsement of the Certificates of successful candidates.

Some candidates may take Stage I Typewriting during the course, or progress to this and other Stage I examinations or the Diploma in Office Procedures.

London Chamber of Commerce and Industry

Marlowe House, Station Road, Sidcup, Kent DA15 7BJ
01-309 0440

Secretarial Studies Certificate

This incorporates the Word Processing Group Award, Shorthand-Typist and Audio-Typist Certificates. Candidates must pass in Communication (Use of English and Secretarial Transcription – Shorthand and/or Audio); Office Procedures; and Background to Business. The optional component is Word Processing, for the Secretarial Studies Certificate with Word Processing.

Candidates who fail to gain the full award will be awarded single-subject certificates for those subjects passed. A candidate who passes Use of English and Secretarial Transcription and Word Processing will be awarded the Word Processing Group Certificate. A candidate who passes in Use of English and Secretarial Transcription will be awarded the Shorthand-Typist Certificate and/or Audio-Typist Certificate, as appropriate.

Entry to the examination normally follows an approved course of study and is appropriate for the following categories of student:

1. Holders of GCSE/GCE O level or equivalent qualifications.
2. Those employed as secretaries to members of junior management.
3. Those employed in clerical posts who want to become secretaries.

Private Secretary's Certificate

Candidates must pass in Communication (Use of English and

Secretarial Transcription – Shorthand and/or Audio); Office Organisation and Secretarial Procedures; Structure of Business; Interview. There is also an option in Information Processing.

Candidates who fail to gain the full award, but who pass in Use of English and Secretarial Transcription are awarded the Shorthand-Typist Certificate and/or Audio-Typist Certificate, as appropriate.

Candidates should normally be 18 in the year in which they take the examination.

Entry to the examination normally follows an approved course of study and is appropriate for the following categories of student:

1. Holders of the Secretarial Studies Certificate.
2. Holders of GCE A level, GCSE/GCE O level, or equivalent qualifications.
3. People employed as secretaries to members of middle management.

Private and Executive Secretary's Diploma
Candidates must pass in Communication (Use of English; Meetings; Secretarial Transcription – Shorthand and/or Audio); Secretarial Administration; Management Appreciation; Interview. There is also an option in Information Processing.

Candidates who fail to gain the full award, but who pass the option in Information Processing are awarded a single-subject certificate. A candidate who fails the full diploma but passes in Use of English, Secretarial Transcription and Information Processing is awarded the Information Processing Group Diploma. Those who fail the full diploma but pass in the Use of English and Secretarial Transcription are awarded the Shorthand-Typist Diploma and/or Audio-Typist Diploma.

Candidates should normally be not less than 20 in the year in which the examination is taken.

Entry
Entry to the examination normally follows an approved course of study and is appropriate for the following categories of student:

1. Holders of the Private Secretary's Certificate.
2. Holders of GCE A level, advanced, or graduate qualifications.
3. Mature persons holding positions of secretarial and administrative responsibility.

Secretarial Language Certificate

Available in French, German and Spanish. Candidates must pass the three parts: Part I, Translation and Summary; Part II, Secretarial Skills; Part III, Oral Test.

The Secretarial Language Certificate is suitable for one-year courses for students who already hold a good GCSE/GCE O level in the language, or two-year post GCSE/GCE O level courses where a higher qualification is not considered suitable.

Advanced Secretarial Language Certificate

Available in French, German and Spanish. Candidates must pass the three parts: Part 1, Translation and Summary; Part II, Secretarial Skills; Part III, Oral Test.

The Advanced Secretarial Language Certificate is suitable for one-year courses for students who already hold GCE A level in the language (or the Secretarial Language Certificate). It is also suitable for two-year courses for students who already hold a good GCSE/GCE O level in the language.

Secretarial Language Diploma

Available in French, German and Spanish. Candidates must pass the three parts: Part I, Translation, Summary and Report; Part II, Secretarial Skills; Part III, Oral Test.

The Secretarial Language Diploma is suitable for the executive secretarial student with a high level of language competence, ie for students with graduate (or equivalent) qualifications in the language or for holders of the Advanced Secretarial Language Certificate. The Diploma qualification is also suitable for foreign students with a native command of the relevant language.

Single-Subject Certificates

First Level (formerly Elementary Stage)
Audio-Typewriting (series 3); Bookkeeping (All series); Elements of Commerce (Series 3); English for Business (Series 2, 3 and 4); English for Commerce (All series); Handwriting (Series 3); Mathematics (Series 3); Office Practice (Series 2 and 3); Shorthand (English; 50 and 60 wpm) (All series); Shorthand (French; 50 and 60 wpm) (Series 2); Typewriting (All series).

Second Level (formerly Intermediate Stage)
Audio-Typewriting (Series 3); Bookkeeping and Accounts (All series); Business Calculations (Series 2, 3 and 4); English for Commerce (All series); English for Business (Series 2, 3 and 4);

Office Practice (Series 3); Shorthand (English; 70 and 80; 90 and 100 wpm) (All series); Shorthand (French; 70, 80, 90 and 100 wpm) (Series 2); Structure of Commerce (Series 2, 3 and 4); Typewriting (All series); Word Processing (Series 2 and 4).

Third Level (formerly Higher Stage)
Business Computing (Series 2 and 4); Commerce and Finance (Series 2 and 4); English for Business (Series 2, 3 and 4); English for Commerce (Series 2, 3 and 4); Information Processing (Series 2); Shorthand (English; 110 and 120 wpm, Series 2 and 3; 130 and 140 wpm, Series 2); Typewriting (All series).

Note: English for Business is an acceptable alternative to English for Commerce for the First Level Group Certificate in Shorthand and Typewriting and the Second Level Group Certificate in Shorthand and Typewriting.

A Practical Word Processing Test is available at a number of examination centres approved by the LCCI. A set of assignments will be used to test the candidate's ability to carry out the specified functions. Each candidate who passes all assignments plus an interview and further tests will gain a certificate naming the type of equipment used, and listing the functions covered. The test will be available at any time of the year and is suitable for concentrated short training courses run by training agencies or the MSC.

Colleges in the United Kingdom
Secretarial courses are offered for the following examinations:

Secretarial Studies Certificate (S)
Private Secretary's Certificate (C)
Private and Executive Secretary's Diploma (D)
Secretarial Language Certificates (L).

Colleges approved for Word and Information Processing options are indicated: W and I.

S		W	**Aberdare**, College of Further Education
S			**Aberystwyth**, Ceredigion College of Further Education
S	C		**Abingdon**, Abingdon College of Further Education
S		W	**Accrington**, Accrington and Rossendale College of Further Education
S	C		**Alton**, Alton College
S			**Altrincham**, South Trafford College of Further Education
	C	D	**Amersham**, Amersham College of Further Education, Art and Design

58 *Careers in Secretarial and Office Work*

	C				**Antrim**, Technical College
S	C	D		W/I	**Armagh**, College of Further Education
S					**Armley**, Leeds Special Centre
S	C				**Ashford**, Spelthorne College
S	C				**Ashington**, Northumberland City Technical College
S	C		L	W/I	**Ashton-under-Lyne**, Tameside College of Technology
S	C				**Aylesbury**, Aylesbury College of Further Education
S	C				**Banbury**, North Oxfordshire Technical College
	C	D		W/I	**Bangor**, Northdown College of Further Education
	C			I	**Barnet**, College of Further Education
S				W	**Barnsley**, Barnsley College of Technology
S					**Barnstaple**, North Devon College
S	C	D			**Barrow-in-Furness**, College of Further Education
S	C				**Barry**, College of Further Education
S	C		L	W	**Basildon**, Basildon College of Further Education
S				W	**Basildon**, Fryerns School
S	C			W	**Basingstoke**, Basingstoke Technical College
S	C				**Bath**, Camden Secretarial College
S	C			W/I	**Bath**, City of Bath Technical College
S	C				**Beaconsfield**, Secondary/Beaconsfield High School
		D		I	**Bedford**, Bedford College of Higher Education
S			L		**Bedford**, Hastingsbury School
S	C		L		**Belfast**, College of Business Studies
	C			I	**Belfast**, Castlereagh College of Further Education
S					**Belfast**, Rupert Stanley College
S	C			W/I	**Beverley**, Beverley College of Further Education
S	C			W/I	**Bexleyheath**, Bexleyheath School
S					**Bexleyheath**, St Catherine's School
S					**Billericay**, Billericay School
S	C			W/I	**Birmingham**, Bournville College of Further Education
S		D		W/I	**Birmingham**, Matthew Boulton Technical College
S					**Birmingham**, Sir Wilfred Martineau School
S	C				**Bishop Auckland**, Bishop Auckland Technical College
S	C	D	L		**Blackburn**, College of Technology and Design
S					**Blackburn**, St Mary's Sixth Form College
S	C	D		W/I	**Blackpool**, Blackpool & Fylde College of Further and Higher Education
S	C	D			**Bournemouth**, Management International College
S	C			W/I	**Bolton**, Bolton Metropolitan College
S	C			W/I	**Bootle**, The Hugh Baird College of Technology
S	C				**Boston**, College of Further Education
S	C	D	L	W/I	**Bournemouth**, Bournemouth and Poole College of Further Education
S	C	D			**Bournemouth**, Management International College
S	C		L	W/I	**Bracknell**, Bracknell College of Further Education
S	C				**Braintree**, Braintree College of Further Education
S	C			W/I	**Bridgend**, Bridgend College of Technology
S				W	**Bridlington**, East Yorkshire College of Further Education
S	C		L	I	**Brighton**, Brighton College of Technology
S	C			W/I	**Bristol**, Filton Technical College
S	C			W/I	**Bristol**, Soundwell Technical College
	C				**Bristol**, South Bristol Technical College
S	C	D		W/I	**Brockenhurst**, Brockenhurst VI Form College
S			L		**Bromley**, Bonus Pastor RC School
S	C	D		W/I	**Bromley**, Bromley College of Technology
				W	**Bromley**, Hayes School
S	C	D	L	W/I	**Bromsgrove**, North Worcestershire College

Qualifications and Courses Available 59

S	C			**Broxbourne**, East Herts College
	C	D	I	**Burton-upon-Trent** Technical College
S	C			**Bury**, Bury Metropolitan College of Further Education
S	C		W/I	**Bury St Edmunds**, West Suffolk College of Further Education
S				**Bushey**, St Margaret's School
S	C		I	**Cambridge**, Cambridge Secretarial College
S			W	**Cambridge**, College of Further Education
S	C			**Cannock**, Cannock Chase Technical College
	C	L	I	**Carlow**, Regional Technical College
S			W	**Carmarthen**, College of Technology and Art
S	C			**Carshalton**, Carshalton College of Further Education
S	C		W/I	**Castleford**, Wakefield District College (Whitwood Centre)
	C			**Chelmsford**, Chelmsford College of Further Education
S			W	**Chelmsford**, New Hall School
S	C	D	W	**Cheltenham**, Gloucester College of Arts and Technology
S	C	D		**Chester**, West Cheshire College of Further Education
	C	D	W	**Chester**, Newton Secretarial School
S	C			**Chesterfield**, College of Technology and Arts
	C	D		**Chichester**, Chichester College of Technology
S	C		W	**Chippenham**, Chippenham Technical College
S				**Chislehurst**, Bullers Wood School for Girls
S	C			**Cinderford**, Royal Forest of Dean College
	C			**Cirencester**, Deer Park School
S	C	D		**Colchester**, Colchester Institute
S	C	D	W/I	**Colwyn Bay**, Llandrillo Technical College
S				**Consett**, Consett Technical College
S	C		W/I	**Corby**, Tresham College (Corby Centre)
	C	D	L	W/I	**Coventry**, Coventry Technical College
	C			**Coventry**, Henley College of Further Education
				Coventry, Hereward College of Further Education
S	C			**Coventry**, Tile Hill College of Further Education
S	C			**Cranbrook**, Jersey House Secretarial College
S	C	D	L	W/I	**Crawley**, Crawley College of Technology
S	C		W/I	**Crewe**, South Cheshire College
S		L		**Crowthorne**, Crowthorne Secretarial College
S	C	D		**Croydon**, Croydon College
S				**Dagenham**, Parsloes Manor Comprehensive School
S	C			**Darlington**, College of Technology
	C			**Dartford**, North West Kent College of Technology
S				**Daventry**, Daventry Further Education Centre
	C			**Derby**, Derby College of Further Education
	C			**Dewsbury**, Dewsbury and Batley Technical and Art College
S	C			**Dolgellau**, Coleg Merionnydd
S	C			**Douglas**, Isle of Man College of Further Education
S	C			**Down**, Down College of Further Education
	C	D		**Dublin**, College of Commerce
S	C			**Dudley**, Dudley College of Technology
	C			**Dungannon**, Dungannon FE College
S	C			**Dunstable**, Dunstable College
S	C		L	W/I	**Eastbourne**, Eastbourne College of Arts & Technology
	C	D		**Eastleigh**, Eastleigh College of Further Education
S	C		W/I	**Ebbw Vale**, Ebbw Vale College of Further Education
S			W	**Enfield**, Enfield College
S	C	D	W/I	**Enniskillen**, Fermanagh College of Further Education
S	C	D	L	W	**Epsom**, North East Surrey College of Technology

60 Careers in Secretarial and Office Work

S	C	D	L		**Erith**, Erith College of Technology
S	C			W	**Esher**, Esher College of Further Education
S	C		L	W/I	**Evesham**, Evesham College of Further Education
S					**Exeter**, Exeter College
S	C	D			**Exeter**, Tolfree's Exeter Secretarial College
S	C				**Fareham**, Fareham Tertiary College
S	C	D	L		**Farnborough**, Farnborough College of Technology
S		D		I	**Folkestone**, South Kent College of Technology
S	C			W/I	**Frome**, Frome College of Further Education
S	C			W/I	**Gainsborough**, Gainsborough College of Further Education
S	C				**Gateshead**, Gateshead Technical College
S	C	D		W	**Gloucester**, Gloucestershire College of Arts & Technology
	C			I	**Gosport**, Bay House School
S				I	**Gravesend**, North West Kent College of Technology
S	C				**Grimsby**, Grimsby College of Technology
S	C		L		**Guildford**, Guildford College of Technology
	C			I	**Halesowen**, Halesowen College of Further Education
S	C	D	L		**Halifax**, The Percival Whitley College of Further Education
S	C			W/I	**Harlow**, Harlow Technical College
S					**Harpenden**, Roundwood Park School
	C				**Harrogate**, Harrogate College of Further Education
	C	D	L		**Harrow**, Harrow College of Higher Education
S	C		L	W/I	**Hastings**, Hastings College of Arts & Technology
S	C		L	W/I	**Havant**, South Downs College of Further Education
S	C			W/I	**Haverfordwest**, Pembrokeshire Technical College
S	C	D		W/I	**Havering**, Havering Technical College
	C	D		I	**Heanor**, South-East Derbyshire College of Further Education
S	C				**High Wycombe**, Buckinghamshire College of Further Education
S	C			W	**Hinckley**, Hinckley College of Further Education
S	C		L	W	**Hitchin**, North Herts College
S					**Horsham**, Collyers Sixth Form College
S					**Huddersfield**, All Saints High School
	C	D		I	**Huddersfield**, Huddersfield Technical College
S	C			W/I	**Hull**, Hull College of Further Education
S	C			W/I	**Huntingdon**, Huntingdon Technical College
S					**Ipswich**, Suffolk College of Higher and Further Education
S	C			W/I	**Isle of Wight**, College of Arts & Technology
S	C		L	W/I	**Isleworth**, Hounslow Borough College
S	C	D		W/I	**Kettering**, Tresham College (Kettering Centre)
S	C			W	**Kidderminster**, Kidderminster College of Further Education
	C			I	**King's Lynn**, Norfolk College of Arts and Technology
	C			I	**Kingston-upon-Thames**, Kingston College of Further Education
S	C				**Lancaster**, Lancaster and Morecombe College of Further Education
S				W	**Leamington Spa**, Mid-Warwickshire College of Further Education
	C	D		I	**Leeds**, Park Lane College of Further Education
S	C		L	W/I	**Leicester**, Charles Keene College of Further Education
	C				**Leicester**, Coalville Technical College
S	C				**Lewes**, Lewes Technical College
	C				**Limavady**, Limavady Technical College
S	C				**Lincoln**, Lincoln College of Technology

Qualifications and Courses Available 61

	C		I	**Lisburn**, Lisburn Technical College
S				**Liverpool**, Huyton College
S	C			**Liverpool**, Kirkby College of Further Education
S	C	L		**Liverpool**, Millbrook College of Commerce
S	C		W/I	**Llandrindod Wells**, Radnor College of Further Education
S	C	D	W/I	**Londonderry**, North West College of Technology
S	C	L	I	**Loughborough**, Loughborough Technical College
S			W	**Loughton**, Loughton College of Further Education
S	C		W/I	**Lowestoft**, Lowestoft College of Further Education
S	C	D	W/I	**Ludlow**, Ludlow and District Training Organisation
	C		I	**Lurgan**, Lurgan College of Further Education
	C	D	L	**Luton**, Barnfield College of Further Education
	C			**Luton**, Luton College of Higher Education
S	C			**Macclesfield**, Macclesfield College of Further Education
S				**Middlesex**, Featherstone High School, Southall
S	C		I	**Magherafelt**, College of Further Education
S	C		W/I	**Maindenhead**, Windsor and Maidenhead College
S	C	L	W/I	**Maidstone**, Mid-Kent College of Higher and Further Education
S	C			**Manchester**, Loreto Sixth Form College
S		D	L W/I	**Manchester**, Central College – St John's Centre
S	C		W/I	**Mansfield**, West Notts College of Further Education
S	C			**Melton Mowbray**, Melton Mowbray College of Further Education
S			W	**Merthyr Tydfil**, Merthyr Tydfil Technical College
S	C	D		**Middlesbrough**, Kirby College of Further Education
	C	D	L I	**Middlesbrough**, Teesside Polytechnic
S	C			**Newbury**, Newbury College of Further Education
	C			**Newcastle under Lyme**, College of Further Education and School of Art
S	C	L		**Newcastle upon Tyne**, College of Arts and Technology
S	C	D	W	**Newport**, Newport College of Further Education
	C			**Newry**, Newry College of Further Education
	C			**Newtownabbey**, Newtownabbey Technical College
S	C		W/I	**Newton-le-Willows**, Newton-le-Willows College of Further Education
	C	D		**Northampton**, Nene College
S			W	**Northampton**, Northampton College of Further Education
S				**North Ferriby**, South Hunsley School
S	C	L		**Northwich**, Mid-Cheshire Central College of Further Education
S				**Norwich**, Norwich & Norfolk Chamber of Commerce and Industry
	C			**Norwich**, Norwich City College of Further and Higher Education
S			W	**Nottingham**, Arnold and Carlton College of Further Education
S	C		W/I	**Nottingham**, Basford Hall College of Further Education
S	C			**Nottingham**, Broxtowe College of Further Education
	C	D		**Nottingham**, Clarendon College of Further Education
S	C		W/I	**Nottingham**, South Nottinghamshire College of Further Education
S	C	L	W/I	**Nuneaton**, North Warwickshire College of Technology and Art
	C			**Omagh**, Omagh Technical College
S	C		W/I	**Orpington**, Orpington College of Further Education

	C				**Oxford**, Oxford & County Secretarial College Ltd
S	C				**Oxford**, Oxford College of Further Education
S	C	D	C	L	W/I	**Oxford**, Wolsey Hall Tutorial College
S	C			L	W/I	**Peterborough**, Peterborough Technical College
S	C	D			W/I	**Plymouth**, Plymouth College of Further Education
S	C				W/I	**Pontypridd**, Pontypridd Technical College
S	C	D	L	W/I	**Poole**, Bournemouth and Poole College of Further Education
S	C	D				**Portsmouth**, Highbury College of Technology
S						**Portsmouth**, Sixth Form College
S						**Port Talbot**, Afan College
S	C		L			**Preston**, Runshaw Tertiary College
S	C					**Preston**, The WR Tuson College
S	C			W		**Radstock**, Norton Radstock College
	C					**Ramsgate**, Thanet Technical College
S	C			W		**Redcar**, Cleveland Technical College
S						**Redditch**, Redditch College
S	C		L	W/I		**Redruth**, Cornwall College of Further and Higher Education
S	C			W/I		**Rochdale**, Rochdale Technical College
S	C	D				**Romford**, Barking College of Technology
S						**Romford**, Marshall Park Upper School
S	C			W/I		**Romford**, Redbridge Technical College
S						**Rossendale**, Accrington & Rossendale College
	C			I		**Rotherham**, Rotherham College of Arts & Technology
S	C			W/I		**Rugby**, East Warwickshire College of Further Education
	C		L			**St Albans**, St Albans College
S	C	D		W		**St Helens**, St Helens College of Technology
S						**St Saviour**, Highlands College of Further Education
	C	D		I		**Salford**, Salford College of Technology
S	C	D	L			**Salisbury**, Salisbury College of Technology
S	C					**Salisbury**, La Retraite Convent School
S	C			W/I		**Scarborough**, Scarborough Technical College
S	C			W		**Scunthorpe**, North Lindsey College of Technology
S	C	D	L	W/I		**Sheffield**, Richmond College of Further Education
	C					**Sheffield**, Stannington College
S						**Sheffield**, Stocksbridge School
	C			I		**Shrewsbury**, Shrewsbury College of Arts & Technology
	C					**Slough**, Langley College of Further Education
S	C		L			**Slough**, St Bernard's Convent School
S	C		L	W/I		**Solihull**, Solihull College of Technology
S	C			W/I		**Southampton**, St Anne's Convent School
	C		L			**Southampton** Institute of Higher Education
	C					**Southampton**, Itchen College
S	C					**Southampton**, Southampton Technical College
S	C			W/I		**Southend**, Southend College of Technology
S	C		L	W/I		**Southport**, Southport College of Arts & Technology
	C			I		**South Tyneside**, South Tyneside College
S						**South Woodham Ferrers**, William de Ferrers School
S	C	D	L	W		**Stafford**, Stafford College of Further Education
	C					**Staines**, Spelthorne Adult Educational Institute
S	C	D		W/I		**Stevenage**, Stevenage College
		D	L	I		**Stockport**, Stockport College of Technology
S	C		L			**Stockton/Billingham**, Stockton/Billingham Technical College
S	C	D		W/I		**Stoke on Trent**, Cauldon College of Further Education
S	C					**Stourbridge**, Stourbridge College of Technology and Art
S				W		**Stratford-upon-Avon**, South Warwickshire College of

Qualifications and Courses Available 63

					Further Education
S			W		**Stroud**, Mid-Gloucestershire Technical College
	C				**Sunderland**, Monkwearmouth College of Further Education
S	C	D		W/I	**Sutton Coldfield**, Sutton Coldfield College of Further Education
S			W		**Swansea**, Swansea College
	C				**Swansea**, West Glamorgan Institute of Higher Education
	C	D			**Swindon**, Swindon College
S	C				**Tamworth**, Tamworth College of Further Education
S	C		L	W/I	**Taunton**, Somerset College of Arts and Technology
S	C			W/I	**Telford**, Telford College of Arts & Technology
S					**Thetford**, Sixth Form Centre
S	C	D	L		**Tiverton**, East Devon College of Further Education
S	C	D	L		**Tonbridge**, West Kent College of Further Education
S	C		L		**Torquay**, South Devon College of Arts & Technology
S	C				**Trowbridge**, Trowbridge Technical College
S	C				**Twickenham**, Richmond upon Thames College
S	C	D	L	W/I	**Uxbridge**, Uxbridge Technical College
S	C			W/I	**Wakefield**, Wakefield College of Technology
S					**Wallsend**, North Tyneside College of Further Education
S	C	D		W/I	**Walsall**, Walsall College of Technology
S	C	D			**Ware**, Ware College
S				W	**Warley**, Warley College of Technology
S	C	D	L	W/I	**Warrington**, North Cheshire College
S	C		L		**Watford**, Cassio College
S				W	**Wellingborough**, Wellingborough College
S	C	D	L	W/I	**Welwyn Garden City**, De Havilland College
S	C			W/I	**Welwyn Garden City**, The Sir Frederic Osborn School
S	C	D		W/I	**West Bromwich**, West Bromwich College of Commerce & Technology
S			L		**Westcliff-on-Sea**, Southend Chamber of Trade and Industry
S					**Weston-super-Mare**, Weston-super-Mare Technical College
S	C	D	L	W/I	**Weybridge**, Brooklands Technical College
S	C	D		I	**Weymouth**, Weymouth Tertiary College
S	C			W/I	**Widnes**, Halton College of Further Education
S		D	L	W	**Wigan**, Wigan College of Technology
	C			I	**Wigston**, Wigston College of Further Education
S				W	**Windsor**, Windsor and Maidenhead College
	C				**Wirral**, Wirral Grammar School for Girls
	C				**Wirral**, Upton Hall Convent School
S	C				**Wirral**, Wirral Metropolitan College
	C			I	**Wisbech**, Isle College
S					**Wokingham**, The Holt School
S	C	D		W/I	**Wolverhampton**, Wulfrun College of Further Education
	C				**Worcester**, Worcester Technical College
S	C			W/I	**Worksop**, North Nottinghamshire College of Further Education
S	C	D	L	W/I	**Worthing**, Northbrook College of Design and Technology
	C			I	**Yeovil**, Yeovil College
S	C	D			**York**, York College of Arts and Technology

London Postal Area

S	C		Acton Technical College, Mill Hill Road, Acton W3 8UX
S			City Business College, EC1
S	C		City and East London College, Bunhill Row, EC1Y 8LO

S				Copthall School, NW7
	C	D	I	Ealing College of Higher Education, St Mary's Road, Ealing W5 5RF
S	C		W	Hackney College, N16
S	C	D	W/I	Hammersmith and West London College, Gliddon Road, Baron's Court W14 9BL
S	C	D L	W/I	Hendon College of Further Education, NW9
S	C	D		International Studies Centre, 205 Wardour Street, W1 4PG
S	C	D	W/I	Kingsway Princeton College, WC1
	C	D		Landsdowne College, SW7
S				Leyton Sixth Form College, E10
S			W	London International College, N7
S				Newham Community College, E15
S	C			Paddington College, W9
S				Pitman Central College, WC1
	C			Queens Secretarial College, SW7
S	C	L	W/I	South East London College, Secretarial Dept, Tressillian Building, Lewisham Way, SE4 1UT
S				Southgate Technical College, High Street, N14 6BS
S	C			South London College, SE27
S	C	L		South Thames College, Putney Building, 50–52 Putney Hill, SW15 6QX
S				South West London College, SW17
S				St Francis Xavier Sixth Form College, SW12
S				St Thomas More Roman Catholic School, SE9
	C	D	W/I	Tottenham College of Technology, High Road, Tottenham N15 4RU
S			W	Vauxhall College of Building and Further Education
S	C		W/I	Waltham Forest College, Forest Road, E17 4JB
S			W	Woolwich College, SE18

Pitman Examinations Institute

Godalming, Surrey GU7 1UU; 04868 5311

Single-Subject Examinations

Shorthand

Shorthand Theory (New Era, Stage I and II; Pitman 2000, Stage II)
Shorthand Speed (from 50 to 140 wpm)
French Shorthand
Legal Shorthand (from 80 to 120 wpm)
Medical Shorthand (from 80 to 120 wpm)

Typewriting

Typewriting (Elementary, Intermediate and Advanced)
Typewriting Speed Tests
Typewriting Transcription Speed Test (Shorthand-based; New Era, Pitman 2000 or PitmanScript)
Shorthand-Typewriting (Intermediate: 80, 100 wpm; Advanced:

120, 140 wpm)
Audio-Typewriting (Intermediate: 80, 100 wpm; Advanced: 120 wpm)
Typewriting Transcription Speed Test (Audio-based) (80 wpm)
Keyboarding

Information Processing
Word Processing (Elementary and Intermediate)
Word Processing – Theory and Practice (Intermediate)
Practical Word Processing
Keyboarding (Intermediate)
Practical Data Processing (Elementary and Intermediate)
Practical Computer Communications (Elementary)
Understanding Computers (Elementary)
Arithmetic (Elementary and Intermediate)
Practical Spreadsheet Processing (Elementary and Intermediate)
Basic Commercial Numeracy
Assessment and Reporting
Bookkeeping and Accounts (Elementary, Intermediate and Advanced)
Cost and Management Accounting (Advanced)

Languages
English Language for candidates in overseas countries (Elementary, Intermediate, Advanced)
English as a Foreign Language (Elementary, Intermediate, Higher Intermediate and Advanced)
English as a Foreign Language (Communicative Syllabus)
English as a Second Language (Elementary, Intermediate, Higher Intermediate, Advanced)
English for Business Communications (Elementary, Intermediate and Advanced)
English for Office Skills (Elementary and Intermediate)
Welsh for Office Skills (Elementary and Intermediate)
English for the Secretary; Systematic Notetaking (Intermediate and Advanced)
Foreign Languages: French, German, Spanish (Elementary, Intermediate and Advanced)
French as a Foreign Language (Levels 1 to 4)

Diploma Courses
Clerical and Office Skills (Levels 1 and 2)
Business Information Systems (Three Levels)

Group Certificates

Basic Commercial Group Certificate
The Pitman Basic Commercial Group Certificate is an award recognising a basic commercial competence sufficient for routine clerical employment. To qualify for this award candidates must have satisfied the examiners in the following subjects, at least to the standards shown below, and all the examinations must have been passed within a two-year period:

1. Bookkeeping and Accounts (Elementary) or Basic Commercial Numeracy.
2. Commerce (Elementary) or Office Practice (Elementary).
3. English (Elementary) or English for Business Communications (Elementary) or English for Office Skills (Elementary) or English Language (NCE) (Intermediate) or English as a Foreign Language (Higher Intermediate).
4. Any other Pitman Examination Institute (PEI) subject at Elementary grade or above, excluding Shorthand Theory but including Typewriting Transcription Speed Test (Audio-based).

Commercial Group Certificate
The Pitman Commercial Group Certificate is an award recognising an all-round commercial competence sufficient for routine clerical employment. To qualify for the award, candidates must have satisfied the examiners in the following subjects, at least to the standards shown below, and all the examinations must have been passed within a two-year period:

1. Bookkeeping and Accounts (Intermediate).
2. Commerce (Intermediate) or Office Practice (Intermediate).
3. English (Intermediate) or English for Office Skills (Intermediate) or English for Business Communications (Intermediate) or English Language (NCE) (Higher Intermediate) or English as a Foreign Language (Advanced).
4. Arithmetic (Intermediate) or Understanding Computers (Elementary) or a Foreign Language (French, German or Spanish) (Intermediate) or Typewriting (Intermediate) or Word Processing (Intermediate) or Keyboarding (Intermediate) or Practical Data Processing (Intermediate).

Higher Commercial Group Certificate
The Pitman Higher Commercial Group Certificate is a new award

recognising that level of knowledge in commercial subjects required of the potential office supervisor. To qualify for this award, candidates must have satisfied the examiners in the following subjects, at least to the standards shown below, and all the examinations must have been passed within one 12-month period:

1. Bookkeeping and Accounts (Advanced) or Cost and Management Accounting (Advanced).
2. Commerce (Intermediate) (First Class) or Office Practice (Intermediate) (First Class).
3. English (Advanced) or English for Office Skills (Intermediate) (First Class).
4. English Language (NCE) (Advanced) (First Class) or a Foreign Language (French, German or Spanish) (Intermediate) (First Class) or Commerce (Intermediate) (First Class) or Cost and Management Accounting (Advanced).
5. Typewriting (Intermediate) (First Class) or Audio-Typewriting (Intermediate 100) or Understanding Computers (Elementary) *with either* Arithmetic (Intermediate) or Word Processing (Intermediate) or Keyboarding (Intermediate) or Practical Data Processing (Intermediate).

Basic Secretarial Group Certificate
The Pitman Basic Secretarial Group Certificate is an award recognising a basic secretarial competence sufficient for routine office employment. To qualify for this award candidates must satisfy the examiners in the following subjects at least to the standards shown below, and all the examinations must have been passed within a two-year period:

1. Shorthand Speed (60 wpm).
2. Typewriting (Elementary).
3. English (Elementary) or English for Business Communications (Elementary) or English for Office Skills (Elementary) or English Language (NCE) (Intermediate) or English as a Foreign Language (Higher Intermediate).
4. Any other PEI subject at Elementary grade or above, excluding Shorthand Theory Stage 1 but including Typewriting Transcription Speed Test (Audio-based).

All qualifying subjects will be shown on the Certificate. Should the candidate pass the Typewriting Speed Test at a speed of 35 wpm or above, the Certificate will be endorsed with the certified speed obtained. The Typewriting Speed Test is not a requirement for the award of the Basic Secretarial Group Certificate but simply an optional extra endorsement.

Secretarial Group Certificate
The Pitman Secretarial Group Certificate is an award recognising all-round secretarial ability. To qualify for this award candidates must satisfy the examiners in the following subjects at least to the standards shown below, and all the examinations must have been passed within a two-year period:

1. Shorthand-Typewriting (Intermediate 80) (First Class) or Shorthand Speed (100 wpm) and 20 wpm in the Typewriting Transcription Speed Test (Shorthand-based).
2. Typewriting (Intermediate).
3. Secretarial Practice (Intermediate).
4. English (Intermediate) or English for Business Communications (Intermediate) or English for Office Skills (Intermediate) or English for the Secretary (Systematic Notetaking) (Intermediate) or English Language (NCE) (Higher Intermediate) or English as a Foreign Language (Advanced).
5. Bookkeeping and Accounts (Intermediate) or Commerce (Intermediate) or a Foreign Language (French, German or Spanish) (Intermediate) or Audio-Typewriting (Intermediate 80), or Word Processing (Theory and Practice) or Word Processing (Intermediate).

All qualifying subjects will be shown on the Certificate. Should the candidate pass the Typewriting Speed Test at a speed of 40 wpm or above, the Certificate will be endorsed with the certified speed obtained. The Typewriting Speed Test is not a requirement for the award of the Secretarial Group Certificate but simply an optional extra endorsement.

Higher Secretarial Group Certificate
The Pitman Higher Secretarial Group Certificate is an award recognising all-round secretarial efficiency and supervisory potential. To qualify for the award candidates must satisfy the examiners in the following subjects at least to the standards shown below, and all the examinations must have been passed within a two-year period:

1. Shorthand-Typewriting (Advanced 120) or Shorthand Speed (120 wpm) and 22 wpm in the Typewriting Transcription Speed Test (Shorthand-based).
2. Typewriting (Advanced).
3. Secretarial Practice (Advanced).
4. English (Advanced) or English for Business Communications (Advanced) or English for Office Skills (Intermediate) (First Class) or English for the Secretary (Advanced).
5. Audio-Typewriting (Intermediate 100) or Word Processing (Intermediate) (First Class) or Commerce (Intermediate) or Bookkeeping and Accounts (Intermediate) (First Class) or a Foreign Language (French, German or Spanish) (Intermediate) (First Class) or English Language (NCE) (Advanced) (First Class).

All qualifying subjects will be shown on the Certificate. Should the candidate pass the Typewriting Speed Test at a speed of 50 wpm or above the Certificate will be endorsed with the certified speed obtained. The Typewriting Speed Test is not a requirement for the award of the Higher Secretarial Group Certificate but simply an optional extra endorsement.

Business & Technician Education Council
Central House, Upper Woburn Place, London WC1H 0HH

BTEC, the Business & Technician Education Council, offer nationally recognised qualifications for both school leavers and those already in employment. A wide range of courses is available, including Business and Finance and Computer Studies courses.

Awards
There are four main categories of qualification: First; National; Higher National; and Continuing Education Certificates, Diplomas and Units.

BTEC First Certificate/Diploma
No formal examination passes are required for entry to these courses, but students should be at least 16 years old. Established as a new award in 1986, the First award is available in Business and Finance.
Length of course: Certificate, one year part-time; Diploma, one year full-time or two years part-time.

BTEC National Certificate/Diploma

Students should be at least 16 years old and for most courses will require four GCSE/GCE O level passes or CSE grade 1 passes or an alternative suitable qualification, such as a CPVE with appropriate attainment or BTEC First Certificate/Diploma. Length of course: Certificate, two years part-time; Diploma two years full-time or three years part-time or sandwich study.

Students successfully completing such courses should be capable of using their initiative appropriately in positions of reasonable responsibility within a wide range of business organisations, and should have the ability at least to progress to junior management positions.

In the case of students taking Secretarial Studies options, they would additionally be equipped as competent secretaries with the full range of appropriate skills, in terms of shorthand, typewriting/audio-typewriting and the associated administrative abilities. Therefore, at the age of 18, students are able to take up responsible posts in full-time employment.

BTEC National Awards also meet the entrance requirements for a BTEC Higher National award as well as other higher education courses.

BTEC Higher National Certificate/Diploma

Students should normally be at least 18 years old and hold an appropriate BTEC National award or equivalent qualification or suitable GCE A level passes. These will depend on the individual course and, where a student enters on the basis of A levels, he or she may have to undertake additional bridging studies or a conversion course.

Length of course: Certificate, two years part-time: Diploma, two years full-time, three years part-time or sandwich study.

Students taking appropriate Secretarial Studies options within courses leading to such awards would additionally be expected to acquire the full range of skills and administrative abilities appropriate to executive secretarial responsibilities.

Students accepted on a full-time course leading to a BTEC Higher National Diploma become eligible for a mandatory grant from their local education authority, subject to the usual residence and income conditions.

BTEC Continuing Education Certificate/Diploma and Units
These courses and units are designed for adults, and students should normally be at least 21 years old. Entry qualifications and length of course vary according to the individual course. Students may be admitted to certain of these studies on the basis of suitable experience and proven ability instead of formal qualifications.

Course Content

BTEC First Course in Business and Finance
This offers a mixture of on-the-job education and training with about 35 days' off-the-job learning for a Certificate or 65 days for a Diploma, completed over one or two years respectively. This could be by day-release at a local college, although block-release and in-house training are also possible. Five units of study are required to gain a Certificate, or eight for a Diploma. Three units are compulsory, one of which is work-based, with the remainder being options which may be planned specifically to meet local employment needs.

Core Unit
Working in Organisations: including a study of relationships with employees, clients, customers and the community.

Core Skills
These may include numeracy, communicating, working with others, using information technology, identifying and tackling problems.

Option Units
Finance, information processing, production, sales, sector study, keyboarding, word processing, receptionist/telephonist duties, information transcription (shorthand and audio).

BTEC National Awards
At this level all students study the following:
People in Organisations (double module)
Finance
The Organisation in its Environment (double module)

Courses with a secretarial stream may include:
Secretarial Studies option modules
Audio-Transcription
Keyboarding and its Applications
Secretarial Services

Secretarial Skills (quadruple module integrating Shorthand), Typewriting (including Audio-Typewriting), Transcription Training and Word Processing
Shorthand Transcription (double module)
Typewriting
Word Processing.

Students wishing to acquire the full range of relevant skills (ie typewriting, audio-typewriting, shorthand transcription and word processing) and who have not previously achieved a significant standard in any of these areas should take the integrated quadruple module, Secretarial Skills. The modules Audio-Transcription, Keyboarding and its Applications, Typewriting and Word Processing are intended for students who do not wish to study the full range of skills, and/or for those who wish to build on previously acquired skills.

The modules Audio-Transcription and Typewriting have been designed to follow Keyboarding and its Applications, and may be taken only by those students who have successfully completed this module, or who have achieved a similar standard.

The module Word Processing is designed for students who are concurrently studying (or who are already qualified in) keyboarding and/or typewriting.

The module Secretarial Services is designed as an essential requirement for any student who intends to work as a secretary.

Not all colleges will be able to offer a full range of options. The choice offered will reflect local demands and needs.

BTEC Higher National Awards

At this level colleges devise their own courses which are validated against guidelines issued by the Council which provide for compulsory coverage of the common study areas outlined earlier.

All students wishing to take Secretarial Studies options as part of a course leading to a BTEC Higher National Award are required by the Council to receive thorough development of the full range of abilities appropriate to the executive secretary.

Further information about secretarial studies within BTEC courses is available from local colleges. The Guidelines for many BTEC courses are being revised, and students will be able to get a clear picture of the course content from the individual colleges.

The way ahead with a BTEC qualification

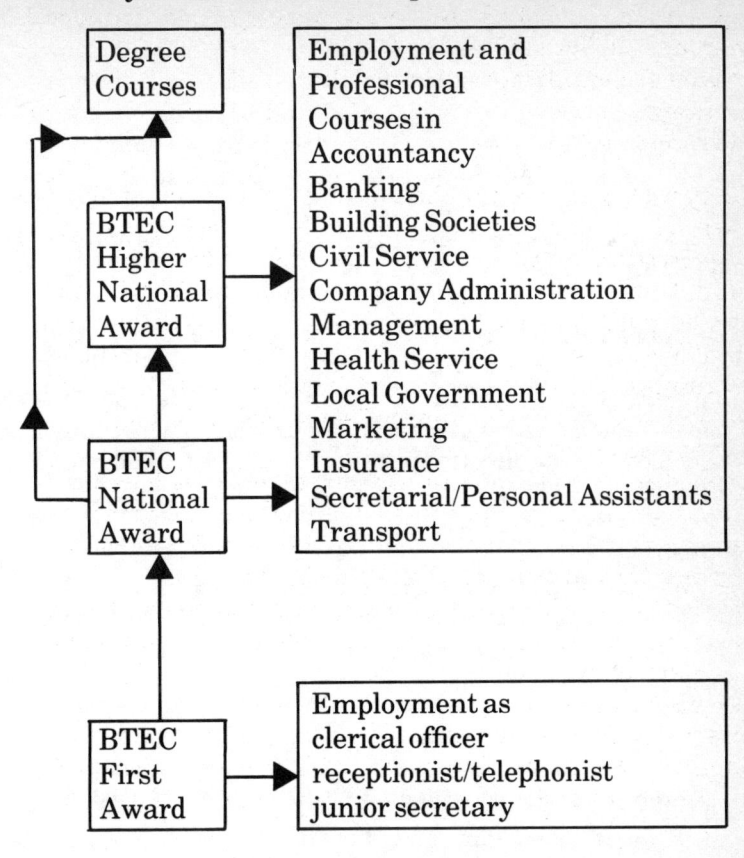

```
┌─────────┐      ┌──────────────────────────┐
│ Degree  │      │ Employment and           │
│ Courses │      │ Professional             │
└─────────┘      │ Courses in               │
     ▲           │ Accountancy              │
     │           │ Banking                  │
┌─────────┐      │ Building Societies       │
│ BTEC    │      │ Civil Service            │
│ Higher  │─────▶│ Company Administration   │
│ National│      │ Management               │
│ Award   │      │ Health Service           │
└─────────┘      │ Local Government         │
     ▲           │ Marketing                │
     │           │ Insurance                │
┌─────────┐      │ Secretarial/Personal Assistants │
│ BTEC    │─────▶│ Transport                │
│ National│      └──────────────────────────┘
│ Award   │
└─────────┘
     ▲
     │
┌─────────┐      ┌──────────────────────────┐
│ BTEC    │      │ Employment as            │
│ First   │─────▶│ clerical officer         │
│ Award   │      │ receptionist/telephonist │
└─────────┘      │ junior secretary         │
                 └──────────────────────────┘
```

> BTEC General Award has been discontinued but is recognised as a qualification leading to BTEC National Award courses

Computer Courses

BTEC Computer Studies courses are designed to suit specific job needs. For example:

If you take a BTEC National Certificate, you will be able either to operate the normal range of computing and data processing equipment or to program in a high-level computer language.

If you take a BTEC National Diploma you will be qualified to do both, because the Diploma covers a wider range of topics.

If you take a BTEC Higher National Certificate or Diploma you will be qualified to assist with the analysis and design of computer systems; write program specifications and program in a high-level language. You can qualify for a career in programming, systems analysis or computer management.

Students should apply to individual colleges for details of their course content.

How to Apply for BTEC Courses
BTEC courses are offered by most colleges and polytechnics throughout England, Wales and Northern Ireland. They are also available in a small number of schools. Application for a place on a course should be made directly to the educational establishment/institution and not BTEC.

Recognition
Many professional bodies recognise BTEC awards for entry/exemption purposes. Universities and polytechnics recognise BTEC National awards as meeting the general requirements for entry to many degree courses. Further particulars may be obtained from BTEC.

Scottish Vocational Education Council (SCOTVEC)

22 Great King Street, Edinburgh EH3 6QH

There are three main categories of award:

National Certificate (NC)
Higher National Certificate (HNC)
Higher National Diploma (HND)

In addition there are post-experience courses including a Diploma for Graduate Secretaries.

Entry Qualifications
National Certificate: this award is available in schools, colleges and other centres to anyone who has attained the minimum school leaving age of 16 years. There are no formal entry requirements. It is a simple certificate which records the knowledge and practical skills acquired by the student in his or her programme of study.

It may be taken:
(a) alongside or as an extension to O Grade, SCE Standard Grade, Higher Grade or Certificate of Sixth Year Studies in the fifth and sixth years of secondary education
(b) on a full-time or part-time basis in a College of Further Education
(c) on a consortium basis with part of the award being provided by a school and part by a college
(d) as part of a TVEI scheme
(e) as part of a Youth Training Scheme
(f) by adults seeking new skills or retraining.

Advanced courses (HNC/HND): These courses are open:
(a) to students who have completed an appropriate National Certificate programme (or its equivalent)
(b) in some cases to students who possess an appropriate group of SCE H and O Grades or GCSE/GCE A and O levels
(c) to students who may qualify for admission on grounds of maturity and experience, at the discretion of the college Principal.

How to Apply
Applications for entry should be made to the centre where the applicant wishes to study.

National Certificate Courses
Programmes are made up of modules, ie units of study. Most modules are of 40 hours' duration. Programmes can include any number and any combination of modules, but will depend on the range offered by the study centre, the vocational employment requirement, if the student is employed, and the possible need to include specific modules for statutory or registration purposes. The National Certificate allows progression to courses in Higher Education and to the advanced examinations of some professional bodies.

There are no longer National Certificates given in specific subjects, but courses are based on the old SCOTBEC qualifications in order to give employers a guideline in estimating the type of courses that students have followed. Courses concentrating on specific skills include compulsory modules which students must gain. Other modules are chosen from a wider selection to make up the number needed in each course which the student must obtain

76 Careers in Secretarial and Office Work

in order to be given the National Certificate Award. Although there are over 2000 modules in all types of subject available, colleges can only offer a limited number; students must approach colleges to find out about the courses and modules they offer. A short Induction Module is offered to help students to select the modules they need. The full choice of modules is given in the National Certificate catalogue.

Students who have successfully completed several modules in either Shorthand or Typewriting will only be credited with two modules as qualifications equivalent to those needed for the former SCOTBEC Scottish Certificate in Office Skills (Secretarial Option), Office Skills (Clerical Option) and Secretarial Studies.

Office Skills (Secretarial Option)

Three modules which must be obtained by all students:
  Communication 3
  Introduction to the Office and General Office Services
  Business Documents and Methods of Payment

Plus a selection of seven 'elective' modules from:
  Typewriting 1–6
  Audio Typewriting
  Employment and Payroll
  Reception 1
  Mathematics: Business Numeracy
  Simulated Office Work 2, 3 and 4 (half or full modules)
  Personal and Social Development
  Environmental Studies in the Local Area
  Learning and Study Skills 1 (half module)
  Personal Presentation A/ and B (half modules)
  Cash Handling
  Word Processing 1 and 2 (half module)
  Introduction to Computers
  Local Economy
  People and Politics.

Office Skills (Clerical Option)

Two modules which must be obtained by all students:
  Communication 3
  Introduction to the Office and General Office Services

Plus a selection of 10 'elective' modules from:

Employment and Payroll
Financial Record Keeping 1–3
Mathematics – Business Numeracy
Simulated Office Work 1 (half or full module)
Reception 1
Keyboarding
Computer Competence
Environmental Studies in the Local Area
Learning and Study Skills (half module)
Environmental Studies in the Local Area
Typewriting 1–6
People and the Law
People and Politics
Cash Handling
Introduction to Distribution
Consumer Studies.

SNC in Secretarial Studies

Five modules which must be obtained by all students:
   Communication 4 (double module)
   Typewriting 6
   Introduction to the Office and General Office Services
   Business Documents and Methods of Payment
   Secretarial Duties

Plus a selection of six 'elective' modules from:
   Reception 1
   Computer Competence
   Word Processing (half module)
   Audio-Typewriting 1 and 2 (half module)
   Simulated Office Work 3 and 5 (half or full modules)
   Understanding Roles and Behaviour (half module)
   Learning and Study Skills (half module)
   Financial Record Keeping 1–3
   Industrial Relations in the Workplace
   Health and Safety in the Work Environment
   Employment and Payroll
   Shorthand 1–4
   Reception 2 (half module)
   Word Processing (half module)
   Office Organisation and Information Processing
   People and the Law/The Legal Framework.

Modules to cover specialist knowledge required by *Agricultural Secretaries* will be devised at local level. See list of colleges on page 107.

Medical Receptionist

    Communication 3 and/or 4
    Introduction to the Office and General Office Services
    Business Documents and Methods of Payment
    Simulated Office Work 4
    Reception 1 and 2 (half module)
    Medical Reception and Records (double module)
    Typewriting 1–4
    Audio-Typewriting 1
    Word Processing 1 (half module)
    Medical Terminology 1 (double module)
    General Medical Practice Fieldwork
    Hospital Fieldwork
    Accident Prevention and First Aid (half module)
    Understanding Roles and Behaviour (half module).

Medical Secretaries

Modules which must be taken by all students:

    Communication 4 (double module)
    Introduction to the Office and General Office Services
    Business Documents and Methods of Payment
    Secretarial Duties
    Simulated Office Work 4
    Reception 2 (half module)
    Medical Reception and Records (double module)
    Typewriting 6
    Shorthand 4
    Audio-Typewriting 1 and 2 (half module)
    Word Processing 1 (half module)
    Medical Terminology 1 and 2 (both double modules)
    General Medical Practice Fieldwork (double, triple or quadruple modules)
    Hospital Field Work
    Accident Prevention and First Aid (half module)
    Understanding Roles and Behaviour (half module).

Higher National Certificate in Secretarial Studies

Aim
This course is designed as a pre-employment course for those aiming at responsible posts in the administration of secretarial services, and for those already in employment the course provides the opportunity to attain high levels of proficiency in the office arts.

Entry Requirements
Candidates must hold three Higher grade passes (including English or other language-based subject) and two Ordinary grade passes of the Scottish Certificate of Education, or the SCOTVEC National Certificate with a minimum of 12 suitable modules (including Communication 4).

In exceptional circumstances applicants aged 21 and over with lesser qualifications may be accepted on the recommendation of the college Principal.

Subject Content
The Certificate will be awarded to candidates who pass examinations in the following subjects:

Communication III
Office Administration I
Typewriting III (or Typewriting II plus Shorthand II, or Typewriting II plus Audio-Typewriting II)

and *two* of the following:

Shorthand III
Office Administration II
Business Information
Business Environment
People and Organisations
Law and the Office
Information Processing
Gaelic III
Modern Language III
Word Processing III.

College Provision
There are many centres throughout Scotland which offer this course

Careers in Secretarial and Office Work

Notes
(a) Students may sit single subjects within this Group Certificate
(b) The course is offered on a one-year full-time or two-year part-time basis.
(c) A student gaining the equivalent of a pass in Typewriting III by means of the combined Typewriting II and Shorthand II for the purpose of obtaining a Group Certificate cannot offer Shorthand III as one of the two optional subjects.
(d) With the introduction of the National Certificate, the equivalence of Typewriting III may be gained by successfully gaining Typewriting module 6 plus one of the following: Shorthand 80 wpm or Audio-Typewriting 2 or Word Processing 2.

Higher National Diploma in Secretarial Studies

Aim
The course meets the needs of students wishing to gain an advanced secretarial Diploma covering secretarial skills and appropriate business and related studies. Opportunities are given in this course to study a modern language.

Entry Requirements
Candidates must hold the Secretarial Certificate
   or the former SCOTBEC SNC or a SCOTVEC National Certificate with a minimum of 12 suitable modules (including Communication 4)
   or three SCE Higher Grade passes (including English) and two Ordinary grade passes.

It is recommended that students taking Modern Language III as an optional subject should hold a pass in that language at SCOTBEC Stage II, or SCE Higher Grade or some similar standard of qualification.

In exceptional circumstances applicants aged 21 and over with lesser qualifications may be accepted on the recommendation of the college Principal.

Subject Content
The HND in Secretarial Studies will be awarded to candidates who pass examinations in:

Year 1
Communication III

Office Administration I
Shorthand
Typewriting

Year 2
Business Information
Office Administration II
Shorthand/Typewriting.

In addition to the above compulsory subjects, students must pass examinations in three subjects from:

Business Environment
People and Organisations
Law and the Office
Information Processing
Gaelic III
Modern Language III
Word Processing III.

The award of a Stage IV Language pass will be endorsed on the Diploma.

Between the first and second years of the course it is recommended that students should spend a period gaining appropriate work experience. All students are required to gain at least one month's relevant working experience during the course and to produce evidence of this to the college.

College Provision
For addresses of colleges see p 84.

Higher National Diploma in Secretarial Studies (with Languages)

Aim
The course meets the needs of those students wishing to take an advanced secretarial course with languages and provides them with a suitable secretarial linguistic Diploma.

Entry Requirements
Candidates must hold the Secretarial Certificate
  or the former SCOTBEC SNC or a SCOTVEC National Certificate with a minimum of 12 suitable modules (including Communication 4)

or three SCE Higher Grade passes (including English or a language-based subject) and two Ordinary Grade passes.

Students must also hold a pass in at least one language at SCOTBEC Stage II standard, or SCE Higher Grade, or some similar standard of qualification.

In exceptional circumstances applicants aged 21 and over with lesser qualifications may be accepted on the recommendation of the college Principal.

Subject Content
The HND in Secretarial Studies (with Languages) will be awarded to candidates who pass examinations in:

Year 1
Communication III
Office Administration I
Shorthand
Typewriting

Year 2
Business Information
Office Administration II
Shorthand/Typewriting.

In addition to the above compulsory subjects, students must pass examinations in two languages at minimum of Stage III. The award of Stage IV Language passes will be endorsed on the Diplomas.

Between the first and second years of the course it is recommended that students should spend a period gaining appropriate work experience. All students are required to gain at least one month's relevant working experience during the course and to produce evidence of this to the college. Students are recommended to spend at least one month in a country whose language they are studying.

Diploma for Graduate Secretaries

Aim
The course aims at providing an all-round understanding of industry and commerce and a thorough training in the secretarial skills for those who have completed a university education.

Entry Requirements
Candidates should be in possession of a degree of a British university or of the CNAA or a degree of a foreign university where supported by evidence of adequate ability in English. A number of degree equivalent diplomas are also recognised for entry purposes but intending candidates should consult the Council. Each potential candidate should be interviewed at the College concerned prior to acceptance in order that suitability for the course may be assessed.

Subject Content
The Diploma will be awarded to candidates who pass examinations in the following subjects:

Office Administration
Shorthand
Typewriting

and *two* of the following:

Modern Language (A) Stage III
Modern Language (B) Stage III
Business Information
Business Environment
Law and the Office
Information Processing
Word Processing III.

A pass in a modern language at Stage IV will be endorsed on the Diploma.

Proficiency Test in Word Processing
The Proficiency Test in Word Processing is now offered at Stage III only. There is no formal entrance qualification although appropriate typewriting ability is implied. The Word Processing Proficiency Test at Stage III is offered as an external subject twice a year and is designed to give employers a guideline in Word Processing. It is optional. Certificates of Proficiency are awarded to successful candidates. They are 'stand alone' awards and do not contribute to the award of a group certificate or diploma.

Single Subject Award for Medical Stenography
This award is available for students taking a Medical Secretarial modular programme or those in employment. The gaining of the

award entitles the holder to proficiency payment. At each speed (100, 120 and 140 wpm) two or three passages will be dictated with an interval of half a minute after each. The passages will vary in length, will be of a medical character, and may include a letter, a report and a memorandum. All transcripts must be typed.

Colleges offering SCOTVEC Full-time and Day-Release Secretarial Duties Courses

Aberdeen College of Commerce, Holburn Street, Aberdeen AB9 2YT (0224 572811)

Angus Technical College, Keptie Road, Arbroath, Angus DD11 3EA (0241 72056)

Anniesland College, Hatfield Drive, Glasgow G12 0YE (041-357 3969)

Ayr Technical College, Dam Park, Ayr KA8 0EU (0292 265184)

Banff and Buchan College of Further Education, Argyll Road, Fraserburgh, Aberdeenshire AB4 5RF (034 625777)

Barmulloch College, Rye Road, Glasgow G21 3JY (041-558 9071)

Bell College of Technology, Almada Street, Hamilton, Lanarkshire ML3 0JB (0698 283100)

Borders College of Further Education, 8 Melrose Road, Galashiels TD1 2AF (0896 57755) and Commercial Road, Hawick TD9 9AF (0450 74191)

Cambuslang College, Janebank, Cambuslang, Glasgow G72 7BS (041-641 6197)

Cardonald College, 690 Mosspark Drive, Glasgow G52 3AY (041-883 6151)

Clackmannan College of Further Education, Branshill Road, Alloa, Clackmannanshire FK10 3BT (0259 215121)

Clydebank College, Kilbowie Road, Clydebank, Dunbartonshire G81 2AA (041-952 7771/6)

Coatbridge College, Kildonan Street, Coatbridge ML5 3LS (0236 25 22316)

Cumbernauld College, Town Centre, Cumbernauld, Glasgow G67 1HU (02367 31811)

Dumfries and Galloway College of Technology, Heathhall, Dumfries DG1 3Q2 (0387 61261)

Dundee College of Further Education, Old Glamis Road, Dundee DD3 8LE (0382 819021)

Elmwood Agricultural and Technical College, Carslogie Road, Cupar KY15 4HY (0334 52781)

Esk Valley College, Newbattle Road, Dalkeith, Midlothian EH22 3AE (031-663 1951)

Falkirk College of Technology, Grangemouth Road, Falkirk, Stirlingshire FK2 9AD (0324 24981)

Glasgow College of Nautical Studies, 21 Thistle Street, Glasgow G5 9XB (041-429 3201)

Glenrothes and Buckhaven Technical College, Stenton Road, Glenrothes

Qualifications and Courses Available 85

South, Fife KY6 2RA (0592 772233)
Inverness College of Further and Higher Education, Longman Road, Inverness, Inverness-shire IV1 1SA (0463 236681)
Jewel and Esk Valley College, Newbattle Road, Eskbank, Dalkeith EH22 3AE (031-663 1951)
Kilmarnock College, Holehouse Road, Kilmarnock KA3 7AT (0563 23501)
Kirkcaldy College of Technology, St Brycedale Avenue, Kirkcaldy, Fife KY1 1EX (0592 268591)
Kirkwall Grammar School Further Education Centre, Kirkwall, Orkney KW15 1QN (0856 2102)
Langside College, 50 Prospecthill Road, Glasgow G42 9LB (041-649 4991)
Lauder Technical College, Halbeath, Dunfermline, Fife KY11 5DY (0383 726201)
Lews Castle College, Stornoway, Isle of Lewis PA86 0XR (0851 3311)
Moray College of Further Education, Hay Street, Elgin, Moray IV30 2NN (0343 3425)
Motherwell College, Dalzell Drive, Motherwell ML1 2DD (0698 59641)
Perth College of Further Education, Brahan Estate, Crieff Road, Perth, Perthshire PH1 2NX (0738 27044)
Reid Kerr College, Renfrew Road, Paisley, Renfrewshire PA3 4DR (041-889-4225/6/7)
Shetland College of Further Education, Gressy Lane, Lerwick, Shetland (0595 5514)
Stevenson College of Further Education, Bankhead Avenue, Sighthill, Edinburgh EH11 4DE (031-453 6161)
Stow College, 43 Shamrock Street, Glasgow G4 9LD (041-332 1786)
Telford College of Further Education, Crewe Toll, Edinburgh EH4 2NZ (031-332 2491)
Thurso Technical College, Ormlie Road, Thurso, Caithness KW14 7EE (0847 66161)
James Watt College, Finnart Street, Greenock, Renfrewshire PA16 8HF (0475 24433)
West Lothian College of Further Education, Marjoribanks Street, Bathgate, West Lothian (0506 634300)

A number of SCOTVEC courses are likely to be available on an evening class basis at most of the above centres and at many other centres not listed. Education Authority offices should be able to provide information on the availability of evening classes in their area. Several Education Authorities publish a prospectus of evening class courses.

The Regional Advisory Councils

These various bodies offer their own examinations and awards as well as those of the RSA, London Chamber of Commerce and Industry (LCCI), Pitmans, BTEC etc. For details of courses offered by individual colleges, write to the council covering your particular area.

86 Careers in Secretarial and Office Work

East Anglian Regional Advisory Council for Further Education
2 Looms Lane, Bury St Edmunds, Suffolk IP33 1HE; 0284 64977
(covering Norfolk, Suffolk, Cambridgeshire, Essex, Bedfordshire)

East Midlands Further Education Council
Robins Wood House, Robins Wood Road, Aspley, Nottingham NG8 3NH

Northern Council for Further Education
5 Grosvenor Villas, Grosvenor Road, Newcastle upon Tyne NE2 2RU; 091-281 3242

North Western Regional Advisory Council for Further Education
Town Hall, Walkden Road, Worsley, Manchester M28 4QE; 061-702 8700

Regional Advisory Council for Further Education, London and South-Eastern Region
Tavistock House South, Tavistock Square, London WC1H 9LR; 01-388 0027
(covering Greater London, Kent, Surrey, East Sussex, Buckinghamshire, Hertfordshire, Essex)

Regional Council for Further Education for the South West
Wessex Lodge, 11–13 Billetfield, Taunton, Somerset TA1 3NN; 0823 85491
(covering Avon, Cornwall, Devon, Dorset, Gloucestershire, Scilly Isles, Somerset, Wiltshire)

Southern Regional Council for Further Education
26 Bath Road, Reading RG1 6NT; 0734 52120 and 52193

Welsh Joint Education Committee
245 Western Avenue, Cardiff CF5 2YX; 0222 561231

West Midlands Advisory Council for Further Education
Norfolk House, Smallbrook, Queensway, Birmingham B5 4NB; 021-643 8924
(covering Shropshire, Staffordshire, West Midlands, Herefordshire, Worcestershire and Warwickshire)

Yorkshire and Humberside Council Association for Further and Higher Education
Bowling Green Terrace, Leeds LS11 9SX; 0532 440751

Specialist Courses
Personal Secretaries
Royal Society of Arts Examinations Board
Colleges where courses leading to the Diploma for Personal Assistants have been approved

Greater London
Barking College of Technology, Lymington Annexe, Lymington Road, Dagenham, Essex RH7 0XU
Bromley College of Technology, Rookery Lane, Bromley, Kent BR2 8HE
Erith College of Technology, Tower Road, Belvedere, Erith, Kent DA17 6JA
Harrow College of Higher Education, Watford Road, Northwick Park, Harrow HA1 3TP
Havering Technical College, Ardleigh Green Road, Hornchurch, Essex RM11 2LL
Kingston College of Further Education, Kingston Hall Road, Kingston-upon-Thames KT1 2AQ
Waltham Forest College, Forest Road, London E17 4JB
West London Institute of Higher Education, Lancaster House, Borough Road, Isleworth, Middlesex TW7 5DU

Avon
City of Bath Technical College, Avon Street, Bath BA1 1UP
Weston-Super-Mare Technical College, Knightstone Road, Weston-Super-Mare BS23 2AL

Bedfordshire
Luton College of Higher Education, Park Square, Luton LU1 3JU

Berkshire
Windsor and Maidenhead College, Boyn Hill Avenue, Maidenhead SL6 4EZ

Cambridgeshire
Cambridge College of Arts & Technology, Department of Business Studies, East Road, Cambridge CB1 2AJ
Peterborough Technical College, Park Crescent, Peterborough PE1 4DZ

Channel Islands
Highlands College, St Saviour, Jersey

Cheshire
Chester College of Further Education, Eaton Road, Handbridge, Chester CH4 7ER

North Cheshire College, Warrington North Campus, Winwick Road, Warrington WA2 8QA

Cleveland
Teesside Polytechnic, Department of Management, Flatts Lane Centre, Normanby TS6 0Q6

Coventry
Coventry Technical College, Butts, Coventry CV1 2DG

Devon
Plymouth College of Further Education, Kings Road, Devonport, Plymouth PL1 5QG

South Devon College of Arts and Technology, Newton Road, Torquay TQ2 5BY

Dorset
Bournemouth and Poole College of Further Education, Lansdowne, Bournemouth BH1 3JJ

Durham
New College Durham, Framwellgate Moor, Durham DH1 5ES

Essex
Basildon College of Further Education, Nethermayne, Basildon SS16 5NN

Chelmsford College of Further Education, Dovedale, Upper Mousham Street, Chelmsford CM2 0JQ

Colchester Institute of Higher Education, Sheepen Road, Colchester CO3 3LL

Harlow Technical College, College Square, The High, Harlow CM20 1LT

Gloucestershire
Gloucester College of Arts and Technology, 73 The Park, Cheltenham GL50 2RR

Greater Manchester
Central Manchester College, St John's Centre, Lower Hardman Street, Manchester M3 3ER

Rochdale Technical College, St Mary's Gate, Rochdale OU2 6RY

Salford College of Technology, Frederick Road, Salford M6 6PU
Tameside College of Technology, Beaufort Road, Ashton-under-Lyne OL6 6NX

Hampshire
Basingstoke Technical College, Worting Road, Basingstoke RG21 1TH
Farnborough College of Technology, Boundary Road, Farnborough GU14 6SB
Highbury College of Technology, Cosham, Portsmouth PO6 2SA
Southampton Institute of Higher Education, East Park Terrace, Southampton SO9 4WW

Hertfordshire
St Alban's College, Hatfield Road, St Albans AL1 3RJ
Cassio College, Langley Road, Watford WD1 3RH

Humberside
Hull College of Further Education, Queen's Gardens, Hull HU1 3DG

Kent
Canterbury College of Technology, New Dover Road, Canterbury CT1 3AJ
North West Kent College of Technology, Miskin Road, Dartford DA1 2LU
West Kent College, Brook Street, Tonbridge TN9 2PW

Leicestershire
Loughborough Technical College, Radmoor, Loughborough LE11 3BT

Lincolnshire
Lincoln College of Technology, Cathedral Street, Lincoln LN2 5HQ

Merseyside
Knowsley Central Tertiary College, Rupert Road, Roby L36 9TD
Millbank College of Commerce, Bankfield Road, Liverpool L13 0BQ
St Helens College of Technology, Water Street, St Helens WA10 1PZ
Wirral Metropolitan College, Borough Road, Birkenhead, Wirral L42 9QD

Norfolk
Norwich City College of Further and Higher Education, Ipswich Road, Norwich NR2 2LJ

Nottinghamshire
Clarendon College of Further Education, Pelham Avenue, Nottingham NG5 1AL

Oxfordshire
Abingdon College of Further Education, Northcourt Road, Abingdon OX14 1NW
Oxford College of Further Education, Oxpens Road, Oxford OX1 1SA

Shropshire
Shrewsbury College of Arts and Technology, London Road, Shrewsbury SY2 6PR

Staffordshire
Burton on Trent Technical College, Litchfield Street, Burton on Trent DE14 3RL
Cauldon College, The Concourse, Stoke Road, Shelton, Stoke-on-Trent ST4 2DG
Tamworth College of Further Education, Croft Street, Upper Gungate, Tamworth B79 8AE

Suffolk
Suffolk College of Further and Higher Education, Rope Walk, Ipswich IP4 1LT

Surrey
Brooklands Technical College, Heath Road, Weybridge KT13 8TT
Carshalton College of Further Education, Nightingale Road, Carshalton SM5 2FJ
Croydon College, Fairfield, Croydon CR9 1DX
East Surrey College, Gatton Point, Redhill RH1 2JX
Guildford County College of Technology, Stoke Park, Guildford GU1 1EZ
North East Surrey College of Technology, Reigate Road, Ewell KT17 3DS

Sussex
Brighton College of Technology, Pelham Street, Brighton BN1 4FA

Chichester College of Technology, Westgate Fields, Chichester
PO19 1SB
Crawley College of Technology, College Road, Crawley RH10 3TB
Worthing College of Technology, Broadwater Road, Worthing
BN14 8HJ

Wales
Aberystwyth College of Further Education, Llanbadarn Campus,
Llanbadarn Fawr, Aberystwyth, Dyfed SY23 3BP
Gwynedd Technical College, Ffriddoedd Road, Bangor, Gwynedd
LL57 2TP
Llandrillo Technical College, Llandudno Road, Rhos-on-Sea,
Colwyn Bay LL28 4HZ
Merthyr Tydfil Technical College, Ynsfach, Merthyr Tydfil, Mid-
Glamorgan CF48 1AR
Newport College of Further Education, Nash Road, Newport,
Gwent NP6 2BR
North East Wales Institute, Mold Road, Wrexham, Clwyd
LL11 2AW
South Glamorgan Institute of Higher Education, Colchester
Avenue, Cardiff CF3 7XR
West Glamorgan Institute of Higher Education, Townhill Road,
Mount Pleasant, Swansea SA1 6ED

Warwickshire
East Warwickshire College, Lower Hillmorton Road, Rugby
CV21 3QS
Mid-Warwickshire College of Further Education, Warwick New
Road, Leamington Spa CV32 5JE

West Midlands
Dudley College of Technology, The Broadway, Dudley DY1 4AS
Solihull College of Technology, Blossomfield Road, Solihull
B91 1SB
Walsall College of Technology, St Paul's Street, Walsall WS1 1XN

Wiltshire
Chippenham Technical College, Cocklebury Road, Chippenham
SN15 3QD
The College, Regent Circus, Swindon SN1 1PT
Salisbury College of Technology, Southampton Road, Salisbury
SP1 2LW
Trowbridge Technical College, College Road, Trowbridge
BA14 0ES

Worcestershire

North Worcestershire College, School Drive, Stratford Road, Bromsgrove

Redditch College, Peakman Street, Redditch B98 8DW

Worcestershire Technical College, Deansway, Worcester WR1 2JF

Yorkshire

Bradford and Ilkley Community Centre, West Brook Buildings, Great Horton Road, Bradford BD7 1AY

Doncaster Metropolitan Institute of Higher Education, Waterdale, Doncaster DN1 3EX

Richmond College, Spinkhill Drive, Sheffield S13 8FD

York College of Arts and Technology, Dringhouses, York YO2 1UA

Northern Ireland

Ballymena Technical College, Farm Lodge Avenue, Ballymena, County Antrim

Belfast College of Business Studies, Brunswick Street, Belfast BT2 7GX

North West College of Technology, Strand Road, Londonderry BT48 7BY

Irish Republic

Waterford Regional Technical College, Cork Road, Waterford

The Association of Legal Secretaries

The Mill, Clymping Street, Clymping, Nr Littlehampton, West Sussex BN17 5RN; 0903 714276

The subjects which are studied and examined are:

The Legal Secretary's Certificate

1. English Law
2. Economics *or*
3. Accounting
4. Office Practice
5. Legal Typewriting
6. Legal Audio-Typewriting *or*
7. Legal Shorthand-Typewriting
8. Word Processing (optional).

The Legal Secretary's Diploma
1. English Law
2. Secretarial Practice and Business Communications
3. The Environment of Business *or*
4. Accounting
5. Legal Audio-Typewriting *or*
6. Legal Shorthand-Typewriting
7. Legal Typewriting
8. Word Processing (optional).

The rules governing the marking of the office skills subjects are not necessarily those of the recognised examining bodies. The importance is that the work produced in the examinations should be of a sufficiently high standard as to be acceptable to the employer. Deliberate errors are introduced into the work to be done which are designed to test the initiative of the candidate. It follows, therefore, that the objective of the college courses should not be to prepare their students to pass the examinations, but to prepare them for work with all the attendant imperfections that this entails.

The Legal Secretary's Certificate is a post-GCSE/GCE O level full-time course and is awarded upon successful completion of five compulsory subjects. Holders become Licentiate Members of the Association and entitled to use the designatory letters LMALS after their name.

Holders of the Certificate may then wish to continue full-time studies for a further one or two years and obtain the Legal Secretary's Diploma which is a post A level qualification and really designed for the future personal assistants in one of the larger legal firms. Diploma courses of one-year full-time are also available for post A level and postgraduate students.

Holders of the Diploma can become Associate Members of the Association and may use the letters AMALS after their name.

The normal entry requirements for these courses are four GCSE/GCE O level passes (grades A, B or C or CSE grade 1) including English for the Legal Secretary's Certificate course and either a pass in the Certificate or at least one A level pass for entry to the Legal Secretary's Diploma.

All courses contain instruction in legal word processing and a period of work experience in a legal office is also a part of the course.

For mature students, such as secretaries who would like to retrain as legal secretaries or existing legal secretaries who want to gain a recognised professional qualification, there are new 24-week part-time courses. These offer training programmes for a Diploma specialising in one of the following aspects of legal work: Conveyancing, Litigation or Probate. Within each specialism there will be four subject areas studied: Law, Secretarial Practice, Word Processing and Legal Shorthand-Typewriting (100 wpm). Examinations will be held in April and June of each year.

Centres Offering Courses Leading to the Legal Secretary's Certificate/Diploma

Amersham College of Further Education
    Stanley Hill, Amersham, Buckinghamshire HP7 9HN
Barking College of Technology
    Lymington Road, Dagenham, Essex RH7 0XU
Barnfield College (Luton)
    New Bedford Road, Luton LU3 2AX
Bromley College of Technology
    Rookery Lane, Bromley, Kent BR2 8HE
Brooklyn Technical College
    Great Barr, Aldridge Road, Birmingham B44 8NE
Bournville College of Further Education
    Bristol Road South, Birmingham B3 2AJ
Cambridge College of Further Education
    Newmarket Road, Cambridge CB5 8EG
Cannock Chase Technical College
    The Green, Cannock, Staffordshire WS11 1VE
Carshalton College of Further Education
    Nightingale Road, Carshalton, Surrey SM5 2ES
Clymping College
    The Mill, Clymping Street, Clymping, West Sussex BN17 5RN
Dacorum College
    Marlowes, Hemel Hempstead, Hertfordshire HP1 1HD
De Haviland College
    The Campus, Welwyn Garden City, Hertfordshire AL8 6AH
Dudley College of Technology
    The Broadway, Dudley, West Midlands DY1 4AS
Elm Park College
    Elm Park, Stanmore, Middlesex HA7 4BQ
Enfield College
    Montagu Road, Edmonton, London N18 2LY
Exeter College
    Heale Road, Exeter EX4 4JS

Erith College of Technology
   Tower Road, Belvedere, Kent DA17 6JA
Halesowen College of Further Education
   Whittingham Road, Halesowen, West Midlands B63 3NA
Havering Technical College
   Ardleigh Green Road, Hornchurch, Essex RM11 2EL
Hounslow Borough College
   London Road, Isleworth, Middlesex TW7 4HS
Huddersfield Technical College
   New North Road, Huddersfield HD1 5NN
Kilburn Polytechnic
   Priory Park Road, Kilburn, London NW6 1YB
Kingston College of Further Education
   Kingston Hall Road, Kingston upon Thames, Surrey KT1 2AQ
Knowsley Central Tertiary College
   Rupert Road, Roby, Merseyside
Llandrillo Technical College
   Llandudno Road, Rhos-on-Sea, Colwyn, Clwyd, North Wales
Ludlow & District Training Organisation
   58 Broad Street, Ludlow, Shropshire SY8 1NH
Macclesfield College of Further Education
   Park Lane, Macclesfield, Cheshire SK11 8LF
Merton College
   Gladstone Road, Wimbledon, London SW19
Mid Cheshire College of Further Education
   Hatford Campus, Northwich, Cheshire CW8 1LJ
Millbrook College
   Bankfield Road, Liverpool L13 0BQ
Nene College
   St George's Avenue, Northampton NN2 6JD
Newcastle upon Tyne College of Technology
   Maple Terrace, Newcastle upon Tyne NE4 7SA
North Cheshire College
   Warrington North Campus, Winwick Road, Warrington WA2 8QA
Norfolk College of Arts and Technology
   Tennyson Avenue, Kings Lynn PE30 2QW
North East Surrey College of Technology
   Reigate Road, Ewell, Epsom, Surrey KT17 3DS
North West Kent College of Technology
   Miskin Road, Dartford, Kent DA1 2LU

96 *Careers in Secretarial and Office Work*

Norwich City College of Further and Higher Education
 Ipswich Road, Norwich NR2 2LJ
Plymouth College of Further Education
 Kings Road, Devonport, Plymouth PL1 5QG
Richmond College
 Spinkhill Drive, Sheffield SL13 8FD
Runshaw Tertiary College
 Langdale Road, Leyland, Preston, Lancashire PR5 2DQ
Sandwell College
 Kendrick Street, Wednesbury, West Midlands WS10 9ER
Scarborough Technical College
 Lady Edith's Drive, Scalby Road, Scarborough, Yorkshire YO12 5RN
Solihull College of Technology
 Blossomfield Road, Solihull, West Midlands B91 1SB
Southampton Institute of Higher Education
 East Park Terrace, Southampton SO9 4WW
Southampton Technical College
 St Mary Street, Southampton SO9 4UR
South Bristol Technical College
 Marksbury Road, Bedminster, Bristol B53 5JL
Southport Technical College
 Mornington Road, Southport, Merseyside PR9 0TT
Southwark College
 The Cut, London SE1 8LE
Stevenage College
 Monkswood Way, Stevenage, Hertfordshire SG1 1LA
Stourbridge College of Technology
 Hagley Road, Stourbridge, West Midlands DY8 1QU
Tameside College of Technology
 Beaufort Road, Ashton-under-Lyne, Tameside, Greater Manchester OL6 6NX
Thurrock Technical College
 Woodview, Grays, Essex RM16 4RY
Trowbridge Technical College
 College Road, Trowbridge, Wiltshire BA14 0ES
Uxbridge Technical College
 Park Road, Uxbridge, Middlesex UB8 1NQ
Walsall College of Technology
 St Paul's Street, Walsall WS1 1XN
West Kent College of Further Education
 Brook Street, Tonbridge TN9 2PQ

Wigan College of Technology
  Parsons Walk, Wigan, Greater Manchester WN1 1RR
Worcester Technical College
  Deansway, Worcester WR1 2JF
W R Tuson College
  St Vincent's Road, Fulwood, Preston, Lancashire PH2 4UR

Association of Medical Secretaries, Practice Administrators and Receptionists Limited

Tavistock House North, Tavistock Square, London WC1H 9LN; 01-387 6005

Diploma and Certificate for Medical Secretaries

To obtain the Diploma, candidates should pass:

(a) Papers I, II, III and IV of the AMSPAR syllabus
(b) RSA Medical Shorthand-Typist's Certificate Stage II (Intermediate)
(c) RSA Medical Audio-Typewriting (Scottish candidates substitute Scottish equivalents).

A Certificate in Medical Secretarial Studies will be issued to candidates who pass Papers I, II, III and IV of the AMSPAR syllabus. Candidates who pass RSA Medical Shorthand-Typewriting Stage II or RSA Medical Audio-Typewriting will have their certificates endorsed accordingly (Scottish candidates substitute Scottish equivalents).

The award of the Certificate in Medical Secretarial Studies may be obtained by undertaking examinations in one or two subjects at a time.

Course Content

Diploma – Syllabus I: Administration and Legal Aspects relating to the National Health Service and Social Services

Diploma – Syllabus II: Medical Secretarial Practice and Office Procedures

Diploma – Syllabus III: Medical Aspects of Secretarial Work. Students should have studied Human Biology to GCSE/GCE O level (or equivalent standard) but candidates who have not done so should have the opportunity of reaching this standard during the course.

Diploma – Syllabus IV: English

Course Entry Requirements
A minimum of four GCSE/GCE O level passes (Grade C or above), one of which must be English Language and normally three academic subjects. (SCE O Grade, CSE Grade 1 and CEE Grade III or equivalent.)

Courses are for two years, but post A level courses of one year only may be run at colleges where a sufficient number of students with the right qualifications would render the course viable.

Mature students may be admitted at the discretion of the Principal. Practising medical secretaries and receptionists unable to attend an approved course of instruction may apply for exemption from the course.

Certificate for Medical Receptionists

The award of the full Certificate may be obtained by undertaking examinations in one or two subjects at a time. A candidate who has passed all papers will be awarded the Certificate in Medical Reception.

Course content
Syllabus I: Administration and Legal Aspects relating to the National Health Service and Social Services
Syllabus II: Medical Clerical Duties
Syllabus III: Medical Aspects of Reception Work
Syllabus IV: English

Course Entry Requirements
A minimum of two GCSE/GCE (academic) O levels (Grade C or above) or CSE Grade 1 and CEE Grade III or equivalents, or mature students at the discretion of the college Principal. It is recommended that full-time students should obtain the equivalent standard of RSA Stage I Typewriting.

Courses run for one year and may be full-time or part-time. Short courses can be arranged for practising medical receptionists.

Diploma in Practice Administration

Course Content
Section A: General Practice Administration
Section B: Legal Aspects of Practice Administration

Section C: Management of premises and the procurement, care and security of equipment, furniture and stores
Section D: Personnel Management
Section E: Communications
Section F: Accounting and Finance
Section G: Data processing, statistics and research
Section H: Project and presentation

Course Entry Requirements
Candidates must (a) be a minimum of 18 years and be employed in general practice and (b) hold the AMSPAR Diploma; or have suitable general practice, nursing, industrial, commercial, public service or armed forces experience and be recommended by their medical employer.

The courses may run for 30 weeks or up to a maximum of two academic years.

College Courses

Medical Secretariat: MS
Medical Receptionist: MR
Practice Administration: PA

Greater London

MS	City & East London College Willen House, 8–26 Bath Street EC1
MS/MR/PA	Hammersmith & West London College Gliddon Road, Barons Court W14 9BL
MS	Harrow College of Higher Education Watford Road, Northwick Park HA1 3TP
MS/MR	North London College 444 Camden Road, N7 0SP
MS/MR	Uxbridge Technical College Park Road, Uxbridge, Middlesex UB8 1NQ

Avon

MS/PA	City of Bath Technical College Avon Street, Bath BA1 1UP
MS	South Bristol Technical College Markesbury Road, Bedminster, Bristol BS3 5JL

Bedfordshire

MS	Barnfield College New Bedford Road, Luton LU3 2AX

MS/PA	Luton College of Higher Education Park Square, Luton LU1 3JU

Berkshire
MS	Bracknell College Sandy Lane, Bracknell RG12 2JG

Buckinghamshire
MS/MR	Aylesbury College of Further Education Oxford Road, Aylesbury HP21 8PD
MS	Milton Keynes College Wroughton Campus, Chaffron Way, Leadenhall West, Milton Keynes MK6 5EH

Cambridgeshire
MS/MR	Cambridge College of Further Education Newmarket Road, Cambridge CB5 8EG
MS	Peterborough Technical College Park Crescent, Peterborough PE1 4DZ

Cheshire
MS/MR/PA	West Cheshire College of Further Education Eaton Road, Handbridge, Chester CH4 7ER
MS/MR	Macclesfield College of Further Education Park Lane, Macclesfield SK11 8LF
MS	North Cheshire College Warrington North Campus, Winwick Road, Warrington WA2 8QA

Cleveland
MS/MR/PA	Stockton/Billingham Technical College The Causeway, Billingham TS23 2DB

Cornwall
MS/MR	Mid-Cornwall College of Further Education Palace Road, St Austell PL25 4BW

Cumbria
MS/PA/MR	Barrow-in-Furness College of Further Education Howard Street, Barrow-in-Furness LA14 1LU

Derbyshire
MR	Derby College of Further Education Wilmorton, Derby DE2 8UG
MS	South-East Derbyshire College of Further Education Field Road, Ilkeston DE7 5RS

Devon

MS/MR	East Devon College of Further Education Bolham Road, Tiverton EX16 6SH
MS/MR	Plymouth College of Further Education Paradise Road, Devonport, Plymouth

Durham

MS	New College Durham Framwellgate Moor, Durham DH1 5ES

Essex

MS/MR	Barking College of Technology Lymington Annexe, Lymington Road, Dagenham, Essex
MS	Basildon College of Further Education Nethermayne, Basildon SS16 5NN
MS/MR	Chelmsford College of Further Education Upper Moulsham Street, Chelmsford CM2 0JQ
MS	Colchester Institute of Higher Education Sheepen Road, Colchester CO3 3LL
MS	Harlow Technical College East Site, The Hides, Harlow CM20 3RA

Greater Manchester

MS	Bolton Metropolitan College G Block, Rydley Street, Bolton BL2 1WH
MS	Oldham College of Technology Rochdale Road, Oldham OL9 6AA
MS/MR/PA	Salford College of Technology Frederick Road, Salford M6 6PU
MS/MR/PA	South Manchester Community College Fielden Park Centre, Barlow Moor Road, West Didsbury, Manchester M20 8PQ
MS	South Trafford College of Further Education Manchester Road, West Timperley, Altrincham WA1 45PQ
MS	Stockport College of Technology Wellington Road South, Stockport SK1 3UQ
MS	Tameside College of Technology Beaufort Road, Ashton-under-Lyne OL6 6NX

Hampshire

MS/MR	Eastleigh College of Further Education Chestnut Avenue, Eastleigh SO5 5HT
MS/MR/PA	Farnborough Technical College Boundary Road, Farnborough GU14 6SB

102 Careers in Secretarial and Office Work

MS/MR/PA Highbury College of Technology
  Cosham, Portsmouth PO6 2SA

Herefordshire
MS/MR/PA Herefordshire Technical College
  Folly Lane, Herefordshire HR1 1LS

Hertfordshire
MS Cassio College
  Langley Road, Watford WD1 3RH

MS East Herts College of Further Education
  Turnford, Broxbourne EN10 6AF

MS/PA/MR North Herts College
  Cambridge Road, Hitchin SG4 0JD

Humberside
MR East Yorkshire College of Further Education
  West Street, Bridlington YO15 3EA

MR North Lindsey College of Technology
  Kinsway, Scunthorpe DN17 1AJ

Kent
MS/MR/PA Canterbury College of Technology
  New Dover Road, Canterbury CT1 3AJ

MS/MR Erith Technical College
  Tower Road, Belvedere DA17 6JA

MS/MR Mid-Kent College of Higher & Further Education
  Oakwood Park, Maidstone ME16 8AQ

MS/MR/PA West Kent College
  Brook Street, Tonbridge TN9 2PW

Lancashire
MS/MR Blackburn College
  Fielden Street, Blackburn BB2 1LH

MS/MR Lancaster & Morecombe College of Further Education
  Torrisholm Road, Lancaster LA1 2TY

MS/MR Nelson & Colne College of Further Education
  Scotland Road, Nelson BB9 7YT

MS/MR Runshaw Tertiary College
  Leyland, Preston PR5 2DQ

Leicestershire
MS Wigston College of Further Education
  Station Road, Wigston Magna LE8 2DW

Lincolnshire
MS Lincoln College of Technology
  Cathedral Street, Lincoln LN2 5NG

Qualifications and Courses Available

Merseyside

MS	Kirkby College of Further Education Cherryfield Drive, Kirkby, Nr Liverpool L32 8SF
MS	Millbrook College (Bankhead Centre) Bankfield Road, Liverpool L13 0BQ
MS/MR	Southport College of Art and Technology Mornington Road, Southport PR9 0TS
MS	The Hugh Baird College of Technology Balliol Road, Bootle L20 7EW

Norfolk

MR	Norfolk College of Arts and Technology Tennyson Avenue, King's Lynn, Norfolk PE30 2QW
MS	Norwich City College Ipswich Road, Norwich NR2 2IJ

Northamptonshire

MS	Tresham College St Mary's Road, Kettering NN15 7BS

Northumberland

MS/MR	Northumberland Technical College College Road, Ashington NE63 9RG

Nottinghamshire

MS	Clarendon College of Further Education Pelham Avenue, Nottingham NG5 1AL

Shropshire

MS	Oswestry College of Further Education College Road, Oswestry SY11 2SA
MS/MR	Shrewsbury College of Art and Technology London Road, Shrewsbury SY2 6PR

Somerset

MS	Bridgwater College Broadway, Bridgwater TA6 5HW

Staffordshire

MS/MR/PA	Cauldon College of Further Education The Concourse, Stoke Road, Shelton Stoke on Trent ST4 2DG
MS/PA	Cannock Chase Technical College Stafford Road, Cannock WS11 2AE

Suffolk

MS/MR/PA	Suffolk College of Higher and Further Education Rope Walk, Ipswich IP4 1LT

Surrey

MS	Brooklands Technical College Heath Road, Weybridge, Surrey KT13 8TT
MS/MR/PA	Carshalton College of Further Education Nightingale Road, Carshalton SM5 2EJ
MS	North East Surrey College of Technology Reigate Road, Ewell KT17 3DS

Sussex

MS	Crawley College of Technology College Road, Crawley RH10 1NR
MS	Eastbourne College of Arts and Technology St Anne's Road, Eastbourne BN21 2HS
MS/MR/PA	Lewes Technical College Mountfield Road, Lewes BN7 2XH
MS/MR/PA	Northbrook College of Further Education Broadwater Road, Worthing BN14 8HJ

Tyne and Wear

MS/MR/PA	College of Arts and Technology Maple Terrace, Newcastle upon Tyne NE4 7SA
MS	Monkwearmouth College of Further Education Swan Street, Sunderland SR5 1EB

Wales

MS/MR/PA	Afan College Margam, Port Talbot, West Glamorgan SA13 2AL
MS	Barry College of Further Education Colcot Road, Barry, South Glamorgan CF6 8YJ
MS/MR/PA	Crosskeys College Risca Road, Crosskeys, Gwent NP1 7ZA
MS	Llandrillo Technical College Llandudno Road, Rhos-on-Sea, Colwyn Bay, Clwyd LL28 4HZ
MS	North East Wales Institute of Higher Education Mold Road, Wrexham, Clwyd LL11 2AW
MS	Pontypridd Technical College Ynys Terrace, Rhydfelin, Nr Pontypridd CF37 5RN
MS	Rumney College of Technology Trowbridge Road, Cardiff CF3 8XZ

Warwickshire

MS/MR/PA	Mid-Warwickshire College of Further Education Warwick New Road, Leamington Spa CV32 5JE

MS	North Warwickshire College of Technology and Art Hinckley Road, Nuneaton CV11 6BH

West Midlands

MS/MR	Brooklyn Technical College Aldridge Road, Great Barr, Birmingham B44 8NE
MS/MR/PA	Dudley College of Technology The Broadway, Dudley DY1 4AS
MS	Halesowen College Wittingham Road, Halesowen B63 3NA
MS/MR/PA	Solihull College of Technology Blossomfield Road, Solihull B91 1SB
MS/MR/PA	Sandwell College Kendrick Street, Wednesbury WS10 9ER
MS	Sutton Coldfield College of Further Education Lichfield Road, Sutton Coldfield B74 2NW
MS/MR	Tile Hill College of Further Education Tile Hill Lane, Tile Hill, Coventry CV4 9SU
MS/MR	Walsall College of Technology St Paul's Street, Walsall WS1 1XN

Wiltshire

MS/MR	Chippenham Technical College Cocklebury Road, Chippenham SN15 3QD
MS/MR	Trowbridge Technical College College Road, Trowbridge BA14 0ES

Worcestershire

MS/MR/PA	North Worcestershire College School Drive, Bromsgrove B60 1PQ

Yorkshire

MR	Barnsley College of Technology Church Street, Barnsley S70 2AX
MS/PA	Bradford and Ilkley Community College Great Horton Road, Bradford BD7 1AY
MS	Doncaster Metropolitan Institute of Higher Education Waterdale, Doncaster DN1 3EX
MS/MR	Huddersfield Technical College New North Road, Huddersfield HD1 5NN
MS/PA	Hull College of Further Education Queen's Gardens, Kingston-upon-Hull HU1 3DG
MR	Joseph Priestley Institute of Further Education 71 Queen Street, Morley, Leeds LS27 0PD

106 *Careers in Secretarial and Office Work*

PA	Keighley Technical College Cavendish Street, Keighley BD21 3DF
MS/MR/PA	Park Lane College of Further Education Park Lane, Leeds LS3 1AA
MS/MR/PA	Richmond College of Further Education Spinkhill Drive, Sheffield S13 8FD
MR/PA	Scarborough Technical College Lady Edith's Drive, Scalby Road, Scarborough YP12 5RN
MS	Wakefield District College (Wakefield Centre) Ings Road Annexe, Ings Road, Wakefield WF2 9SD
MS/PA	York College of Arts and Technology Dringhouses, York YO2 1UA

Northern Ireland

MS/MR	Armagh Technical College Lonsdale Street, Armagh BT6 17HN
MS	Belfast College of Business Studies Brunswick Street, Belfast BT2 7GX
MS	Newtownabbey Technical College 400 Shore Road, Newtownabbey, Co Antrim BT3 9RS
MS/MR	North West College of Technology Strand Road, Londonderry BT48 7BY
MR	Rupert Stanley College of Further Education Tower Street, Belfast BT5 4FH

Scotland

MS	Aberdeen College of Commerce Holburn Street, Aberdeen AB9 2YT
MS/PA	Anniesland College Hatfield Drive, Glasgow G12 0YE
MS	Bell College of Technology Almada Street, Hamilton ML3 0JB
MS	The Borders College Henderson Building, Commercial Road, Hawick, Roxburghshire TD9 9AW
MS	Dundee College of Commerce 30 Constitution Road, Dundee DD3 6TB
MS	Inverness Technical College Longman Road, Inverness IV1 1SA
MS	Kilmarnock Technnical College Holehouse Road, Kilmarnock KA3 7AT
MS	Kirkcaldy College of Technology St Brycedale Avenue, Kirkcaldy KY1 1EX
MS/MR/PA	Stevenson College of Further Education Bankhead Avenue, Sighthill, Edinburgh EH11 4DE

Courses for Farm Secretaries

Buckinghamshire
Aylesbury College, Department of Agriculture and Horticulture
Hampden Hall, Stoke Mandeville HP22 5TB; 029 661 3391
BTEC National Diploma (Agricultural Secretary); two-year full-time course
BTEC National Certificate for Farm Secretaries; one-year full-time course
Farming and Secretarial Foundation Course; one-year full-time course

Devon
Bicton College of Agriculture
  East Budleigh, Budleigh Salterton EX9 7BY; 0395 68353
BTEC National Certificate for Farm Secretaries; one-year full-time course

Hampshire
Hampshire College of Agriculture
  Sparsholt, Winchester SO21 2NF; 096 272 441
BTEC National Diploma for Farm Secretaries; two-year full-time course
BTEC National Certificate Farm Secretarial course; one-year full-time course

Kent
Hadlow College of Agriculture and Horticulture
  Hadlow, Tonbridge TN11 0AL; 0732 850551
BTEC National Certificate farm secretarial course; one-year full-time course

Leicestershire
Brooksby Agricultural College
  Brooksby, Melton Mowbray LE14 2LJ; 0664 75 291
BTEC National Certificate for Farm Secretaries; one-year full-time course
BTEC National Diploma for Agricultural Secretaries; two-year full-time course

Lincolnshire
Lincolnshire College of Agriculture and Horticulture
  Caythorpe Court, Grantham NG32 3EP; 0400 72521
BTEC National Certificate for Farm Secretaries; one-year full-time course
BTEC National Diploma (Agricultural Secretaries); two-year full-time course

Northumberland
Northumberland College of Agriculture
  Ponteland, Newcastle upon Tyne NE20 0AQ; 0661 24141
BTEC National Certificate, Farm Secretarial Work; one-year full-time course

Staffordshire College of Agriculture
  Rodbaston, Penkridge, Stafford ST19 5PH; 078571 2209
BTEC National Certificate, Farm Secretarial; one-year full-time course
Farm Recording and Secretarial; 12-week course

West Sussex
West Sussex College of Agriculture and Horticulture
  Brinsbury, North Heath, Pulborough RH20 1DL; 079 82 2394
BTEC National Certificate for Farm Secretaries; one-year full-time course

Wales
The Usk College of Agriculture
  Usk, Gwent NP5 1XJ; 029 13 2311
BTEC National Certificate, Farm Secretarial; one-year full-time course

Scotland
Barony Agricultural College
  Parkgate, Dumfries DG1 3NE; 038 786 251
SCOTVEC National Certificate (SNC) for Farm Bookkeeping, and Recording, Business Management, Farm Computing; day-release course
Elmwood Agricultural and Technical College
Carslogie Road, Cupar KY15 4HY; 0334 52781
SCOTVEC National Certificate for Agricultural Secretaries; two-year full-time course
Angus Technical College
  Keptie Road, Arbroath, Angus DD11 3EA; 0241 72056
SCOTVEC Modular Programme for Agricultural Secretaries; one-year full-time course

Youth Training Scheme (YTS)

The Youth Training Scheme includes training in Administrative, Clerical and Office Skills among its programmes (in one period 23 per cent of YTS leavers went into those jobs). YTS trainees can specify what they want to do and receive training that involves courses in college which can lead to BTEC and other qualifications. Courses include subjects such as Information Technology, Keyboarding, and Information Processing which give the training in computing skills that are important in office work. Many large companies recruit their office staff through YTS.

YTS is open to young people who are already working, as well as school-leavers who are not yet employed. Schemes are run by employers, colleges of further education and training organisations, voluntary organisations and local authorities.

Programmes run by employers include sandwich courses at local colleges. The Youth Training Scheme is government-funded, and the responsibility of the Manpower Services Commission (MSC).

Length of training
Sixteen-year-old school leavers join a two-year training programme with at least 20 weeks' off-the-job training over the two years.

Seventeen-year-olds go into a one-year programme with at least seven weeks' off-the-job training.

Disabled young people leaving full-time education up to the age of 21 are eligible for two years of training with the opportunity of an extra six months in most cases

Eighteen-year-olds who were unable to start YTS earlier, perhaps because they stayed at school to learn English, are entitled to two years' training.

Training Allowances and Travel Costs
Young people on a two-year programme receive £28.50 a week in the first year and £35 a week in the second. Those with a one-year programme receive £28.50 a week in the first 13 weeks and the higher rate of £35 a week for the remaining nine months. Trainees are repaid any travelling expenses of more than £3 a week; those who have to live away from home in order to get their training may be paid lodging allowances to help to cover the cost. There may also be special reductions on rail and bus routes for regular travellers and young people which could help to reduce costs (1987/88 figures).

Working Hours
Working hours on YTS are normally 40 hours per week, with 18 days' holiday per year with pay, as well as public and bank holidays.

Training Agreement
YTS trainees have a Training Agreement which spells out their rights and responsibilities and those of the training organisation; details of pay, holidays and sickness; discipline and grievance procedures, health and safety legislative protection and details of the training programme. 'Model' training schemes have been drawn up which comprise nationally agreed standards of training, including clerical training.

Throughout the YTS training period there is a regular review of progress and trainees receive a certificate at the end of the period which records achievements, examinations taken and qualifications gained. Trainees can leave the scheme at any time, if they wish, or change to a different training programme that they feel may suit them better (careers officers will advise on this).

How to Apply

All YTS places are notified to local careers officers and Jobcentres; and managing agents (who run the schemes) are also free to recruit direct. Guidance and advice are given by the careers service at Careers Offices, Jobcentres and schools; this includes advice on training, and help in transferring to different training schemes. YTS recruitment and selection is arranged by the managing agents; in most cases this involves an interview which both allows possible trainees to decide whether they want the place as well as letting the interviewer assess whether the training on offer is suitable.

All eligible young people have one year from the date of leaving full-time education in which to enter training. Only time on YTS and time spent in full-time education after minimum leaving age can reduce entitlement to training.

Employment Training

A new government training programme replaces the Community Programme, the new and old Job Training Schemes and other training programmes for unemployed adults from September 1988. It is designed for anyone who has been unemployed for over six months and gives priority to those aged 18 to 24 who have been unemployed between six and 12 months and to those aged 18 to 50 who have been unemployed for over two years. There are special arrangements for certain groups of people, including women returning to work and people wanting training in skills needed in high-tech industries or skill shortage areas.

The new programmes provide up to 12 months' full-time training and everyone on the programme is entitled to have at least 40 per cent of their time spent on off-the-job training in colleges, or as provided by employers running projects. Trainees enter the programme through a Restart interview, or by applying to a Jobcentre. Training is directed by a training agent, who places the trainee with a training manager – employer, local authority or other educational or training organisation. Training with an employer will include practical experience and can lead to a recognised vocational qualification.

Trainees receive £10 per week more than their benefit entitlement, or more if they are entitled to Income Support, plus travelling expenses over £5 per week. For single parents, childcare costs of up to £50 per week will be paid for each child. Further information from Manpower Services Commission offices.